PANZER

*The Illustrated History of Germany's
Armored Forces in WWII*

PANZER

The Illustrated History of Germany's Armored Forces in WWII

Dr. Niall Barr and Dr. Russell Hart

MBI Publishing Company

This edition first published in 1999
by MBI Publishing Company,
729 Prospect Avenue, PO Box 1, Osceola, WI 54020-0001 USA

The information in this book is true and complete to the best of our knowledge. All recommendations are made without any guarantee on the part of
the author or publisher, who also disclaim any liability incurred in connection
with the use of this data or specific details

We recognize that some words, model names and designations, for example,
mentioned herein are the property of the trademark holder. We use them for
identification purposes only. This is not an official publication

MBI Publishing Company books are also available at discounts in bulk
quantity for industrial or sales-promotional use. For details write to the
Special Sales Manager at Motorbooks International Wholesalers & Distributors,
729 Prospect Avenue, PO Box 1, Osceola, WI 54020-0001 USA

Library of Congress Cataloging-in-Publication Data available

ISBN 0-7603-0725-3

Editorial and design by
Amber Books Ltd
Bradley's Close
74-77 White Lion Street
London N1 9PF

Editor: Matthew Tanner
Design: Robert Mathias

Printed and bound in Italy

Page 1: King Tigers in Normandy in June 1944.
Page 2: A panzer crew member, Knight's Cross at his neck, on the Eastern Front in 1944.
Note the skull and crossbones collar badge, which was worn by the personnel of armoured
units.

CONTENTS

CHAPTER 1

BIRTH
OF THE PANZERS

From 1934 onwards, the new Nazi German Reich speedily developed a strategic armoured warfare capability, which built upon the German Army's clandestine – and illegal – experimentation of the late 1920s.

Left: A column of Panzer II tanks parade through the streets. The relatively small dimensions of this design is shown by the size of the upper body of the black-uniformed tank commanders.

Above: In the 1920s the Reichswehr got over the 1919 Versailles Treaty banning of armoured vehicles by conducting tactical exercises that used flimsy wood-and-canvas dummy tanks.

The German panzer (armour) arm that transformed the European balance of power during the early years of World War II emerged neither easily nor quickly. The conditions in Germany during the interwar period both hampered and also provided impetus for the development of the world's first, albeit small, armoured force capable of independent strategic operations.

The tank, a British invention, first appeared on the battlefields of World War I. Yet the technical limitations of armour at the time precluded it from exerting anything more than a tactical impact on the 1916–18 battlefields. It was within the interwar German Army that there gradually evolved a radical new concept: rapidly moving armoured forces conducting strategic deep penetration operations

Left: German Sdkfz 232 six-wheeled heavy armoured cars, with command/signals variants visible in the foreground, parade before military dignitaries during the September 1936 Nazi Party Day celebrations.

designed to disorganise and paralyse an enemy. Such a force, the Germans believed, would allow their emasculated armed forces to overcome more powerful opponents, especially Britain and France, before they had time to mobilise their industrial and demographic strength. What gradually evolved – often as much by default as by purposeful design – was the blitzkrieg (lightning war) concept, which allowed Germany to overrun much of continental Europe during 1939-41.

The genesis of mechanised warfare

The roots of this revolutionary new form of mechanised warfare lay in the experiences of World War I, for the 'armoured idea' was a product of the deadly impasse of trench warfare on the Western Front, which had led to the slaughter of a generation of young European men for almost no military gains. These armoured warfare concepts also evolved from the 'Storm Troop' tactics the Germans developed during 1917–18, which finally provided an operational solution to the deadlock created by trench warfare. Based upon speed and flexibility in the attack, élite 'Storm Troop' units, powerfully reinforced with firepower, used infiltration tactics to enter enemy trenches by surprise and overcome them. 'Storm Troops' therefore sought to confuse, paralyse and out-manoeuvre the enemy. Interwar armoured proponents believed that the tank – with its unique combination of firepower, protection and mobility – could perform the 'Storm Trooper' mission, albeit more cheaply and effectively. The tank could also be wedded to the traditional tenets of Prussian strategy, which emphasised deep penetration, encirclement and annihilation – the basic principles that underpinned the failed German Schlieffen Plan of 1914 (this involved a holding operation against Russian forces while the bulk of the German Army attacked France with an enveloping movement through Flanders and Picardy to surround Paris from the west and south; with France defeated, the Germans could then destroy Russian forces in the East at their leisure). To many German officers between the wars, armour appeared as a means to correct both the flaws they perceived inherent in the Schlieffen Plan itself, and also the mistakes the Germans recognised that they had made in its execution.

Below: Armoured cars of the Order Police, or Ordnungspolizei, line up for inspection in the late 1930s. By this time the Ordnungspolizei was part of Himmler's SS empire, and when war broke out a number of polizei regiments were created. They were used primarily in anti-partisan duties in occupied territories, and also assisted the dreaded Einsatzgruppen squads.

Left top: An entire panzer battalion, with Panzer 1 tanks in the lead echelon, manoeuvres in a highly disciplined mass formation in pre-war Germany.

Left bottom: A German half-tracked artillery tractor tows an 8.8cm Flak 18 heavy anti-aircraft gun on a Sonderhänger 201 carriage during a military parade. This particular weapon would go on to become a potent anti-tank gun in World War II, its high muzzle velocity coupled with an efficient and heavy projectile making it an ideal 'tank killer'.

Above: A column of Panzer I Model A tanks parade along a street filled with watching crowds in Germany in the late 1930s, in one of the carefully orchestrated displays of military might used by the Nazi leadership to show the German people and the world the strength of the Third Reich's war machine. These particular vehicles can be distinguished from the Panzer I Model B in that they possess just four pairs of road wheels instead of five.

The evolution of a German armoured force between the wars was no foregone conclusion, however. Indeed, the conditions prevalent in Weimar Germany during the 1920s suggested that any such development remained unlikely. The 1919 Treaty of Versailles which ended World War I reduced Germany to a 100,000-man army, curtailed German weapons development, and banned tank research and procurement entirely. Moreover, the

massive reparation payments the treaty compelled Germany to pay to the victims of its aggression further drained an economy already badly weakened by war. To cap it all, the global economy suffered a period of devastating instability between the wars (though this paved the way for the 1933 political triumph in Germany of the violently militaristic and racist National Socialist party under its demagogue leader Adolf Hitler, which was to benefit the German armed forces).

On the surface, therefore, the interwar climate did not appear conducive to the development of a costly and revolutionary new form of warfare. Yet appearances were deceptive, for the limitations imposed by the Treaty of Versailles compelled the interwar Germany military to innovate. With the German Army incapable of adequately defending the nation against powerful neighbours still smarting from Germany's aggression of 1914, it was motivated to acquire any advantage it could over potential enemies. Consequently, it sought new ways in which a numerically and materially inferior military force could prevail against more powerful opponents. It was in this context that the tank appeared to offer Germany a possible avenue of escape from the nation's political and strategic situation.

The birth of the panzer divisions

Armoured warfare as a concept, however, remained controversial throughout the interwar period, particularly because technological limitations ensured that until the late 1930s armoured theory remained well in advance of the actual capabilities of tanks. This did not prevent a bitter struggle developing between the wars in all

Above: German tanks of the Condor Legion deploy at the bottom of a reverse slope during the Spanish Civil War. In addition to Panzer I tanks, a solitary Panzer I command variant is visible (the second vehicle to the left of the soldier in the foreground). The conflict offered the German Army its first opportunity to test its light tanks in combat, gaining invaluable experience in the process. The war also underscored the Panzer I's tactical shortcomings: its limited firepower and protection.

Western militaries between youthful, daring proponents of mechanised warfare and more conservative officers. It seemed logical to expect that Germany would go the same way as interwar Britain, France and the United States. All of these countries, despite promising experimentation with mechanised forces, ultimately rejected armoured innovation (hardly surprising, as they were the victors and hence slightly complacent) and wedded the tank to the infantry support role, as they had in World War I.

In Germany this did not prove the case and, despite numerous obstacles, in 1935 its army formed three panzer (armoured) divisions. The explanations for such a development are complex. Ironically, the severe limitations imposed by the Treaty of Versailles provided both the impetus for, and the nucleus of, the future German armoured force. Unencumbered by the dead weight of a large conscript force with obsolete equipment, and reduced to a dedicated, martial élite who were determined to regain their honour

and reverse the political consequences of Germany's defeat in 1918, the interwar German Army actually proved a fertile ground for innovation.

Heinz Guderian

The German military intensively examined the World War I battlefield and came to understand it better than anyone else. The lessons that the Germans drew from this conflict – in terms of the superiority of combined arms and of offensive tactics utilising speed, surprise and shock – further promoted the evolution of an armoured force.

The development of a German tank force also relied heavily on key personalities. The father of the panzer arm was Heinz Guderian, though history probably has exaggerated his role to the detriment of other officers who worked alongside him away from the public glare. In 1929 Guderian, having read the works of British armoured pioneers, developed for the first time in the German Army the notion of strategic deep penetration by armoured forces. Yet his radical notions might have suffered the same fate as the British armoured advocate, J.F.C. Fuller, who in the 1930s was exiled to the wilderness, had not Guderian

Right: A good frontal view of a column of four Panzer I tanks – then still termed under the pseudonym LaS I (agricultural tractor I) – on the move in a built-up area during the Spanish Civil War.

Above: A German Panzer I tank in combat camouflage deploys in open grassland. The firepower of this design was limited to just a pair of 7.92mm MG 13 machine guns. This drawback seriously limited the vehicle's tactical value and led to it being progressively withdrawn from frontline service as early as 1940. In Spain, a few Panzer Is were modified to mount a 20mm cannon, though this resulted in a reduction in performance.

worked in an environment more receptive to change than that which existed in Britain between the wars.

Another influential progenitor of the panzer arm was Colonel-General Hans von Seeckt, the Commander-in-Chief of the German Army from 1920–26. It was Seeckt who created conditions favourable for the evolution of the armoured force. He was a firm proponent of mechanisation, for he recognised that the puny German Army had to rely on speed and mobility to offset numerical and material inferiority. In 1919, the victorious Allies allowed Germany to retain its mounted corps because they deemed cavalry obsolete and fit only for domestic policing. But Seeckt transformed the German cavalry into a semi-motorised strategic reserve. Of equal long-term importance was von Seeckt's emphasis on close integration and coordination between combat arms. His determination to evade existing treaty restrictions also saw clandestine German tank research overseas in Sweden and secret trials in the communist Soviet Union, that other pariah state of the interwar international community.

The Panzer I and Panzer II

During the late 1920s, German firms illegally developed the first tank prototypes which the army tested in field exercises. These exercises examined both the theoretical possibilities of future armoured warfare, and also laid the organisational and doctrinal framework for future success. In the 1920s, therefore, Germany gained rudimentary experience of the design and handling of

Right top: A team of four German soldiers man a light anti-tank gun, probably of 37mm calibre, which has been well dug in but only half-heartedly camouflaged. Note the well-sloped gun shield, designed to enhance shot deflection and thus maximise the degree of protection.

Right middle: A Panzer I tank (this particular vehicle is a Model A variant) crosses a water obstacle in northern Spain. Clearly visible in this picture is the distinctive octagonal superstructure and frontal vision ports featured by this tank design, as well as the small size of the turret.

Right: Panzer I tanks of the Condor Legion in combat in open terrain during the Spanish Civil War. The vehicle in the right foreground appears to possess five pairs of road wheels instead of four, and is hence an example of the Panzer I Model B variant. This model also had a more powerful engine.

armoured vehicles. These were small, but vital, first steps on the road to blitzkrieg.

The emergence of the panzer arm also owed a great deal to Lieutenant-General Oswald Lutz, who in 1931 became Inspector General of Motor Transport Troops and made Guderian his chief of staff. This dynamic team vigorously promoted the armoured idea in the face of entrenched opposition. Moreover, the Nazi political triumph in Germany on 30 January 1933 speeded up the gradual mechanisation then underway in the German Army, since Hitler's inherently racist, violent and bellicose world-view facilitated military innovation. The new Chancellor was determined to employ German military might to transform the global balance of power. Hitler's goals – outlined in his 1926 autobiography *Mein Kampf* – included the restoration of a 'Greater Germany' encompassing all ethnic Germans, the acquisition of a central European hegemony, and then a bid for world power status via a brutal war of extermination against the Soviet Union, which would destroy communism and enslave Eastern Europe's Slav peoples. Only such a destiny, Hitler believed, could acquire the 'living space' that was necessary to guarantee the survival of the Nazi 'New Order' for a millennium. Hitler therefore pursued broad rearmament and sponsored military innovation, be it the army's tank force, the German Air Force's Stuka dive-bomber fleet or the German Navy's submarine arm.

Above: A Panzer I command vehicle plunges down an earth slope. The Panzer I command variant possessed an additional crew member to operate the communications equipment that the vehicle carried. Note the highly visible tactical recognition sign on the roof to prevent accidental attacks by the Luftwaffe.

By 1934 Germany had commenced production of two interim light training tanks, the Panzer I and II, and heavier battle tanks were on the drawing boards. The Panzer I was a light, cheap, easy to construct five-tonne (4.9-ton) tank armed with twin machine guns, while the 10-tonne (9.8-ton) Panzer II mounted a 20mm (0.8in) cannon. With actual tanks in production, the Germans formed a Mobile Troops Command on 27 September 1934, and the next month came the establishment of Germany's first armoured formation, the 1st Panzer Brigade. Its personnel were mainly drawn from the Cavalry Mechanised Division raised in the previous year, which had tested the viability of mobile armoured warfare during the 1933 annual exercises. Hitler's 1935 repudiation of the Treaty of Versailles aided these faltering first steps. Immediately thereafter, an improvised panzer division, built around the 1st Panzer Brigade, took part in the summer 1935 annual exercises. Its success led to the activation of Germany's first three panzer divisions on 15 October 1935. From the start these armoured formations were not simply massed-tank units, for alongside their two regiments of tanks were motorised infantry, engineers, signallers, towed anti-tank guns and artillery. Guderian personally took command of the 2nd Panzer Division once it had been formed, which inadvertently removed him from the centre of armoured development.

The panzers in Spain

In April 1937, the German Army went one step further and combined the three panzer divisions in XVI Motorised Corps, creating the world's first mechanised corps designed for strategic operations. Further progress continued in 1938, when the 4th and 5th Panzer Divisions came into being, and when, on 20 November, Guderian finally became the Chief of Mobile Troops. He threw himself into this new job with his typical energy, for much remained to be done, as was demonstrated during 1937–38 by the involvement of German armoured forces in the Spanish Civil War, the annexation of Austria and the occupation of the Sudetenland. The Germans despatched 180 Panzer I tanks to Spain to assist General Franco's Nationalist forces. These proved to be manifestly inferior to the Soviet T-26 tanks, armed with a 45mm gun, fielded by the Republicans. Nevertheless, the Germans gained valuable operational experience in Spain, particularly in the development of a rudimentary system of air-to-ground cooperation.

The unopposed 1938 German annexation of Austria illuminated numerous organisational and operational weaknesses in the panzer arm, particularly supply and maintenance failures that led to nearly one-third of the German tanks employed breaking down

Above: An Italian Carro Veloce 33 tankette motors along a road in Spain. Built in the early 1930s, and based on the British Carden-Lloyd tankette, this three-tonne (three-ton), two-man vehicle mounted a single machine gun. The subsequent 33/11 variant mounted twinned machine guns.

Below: An armoured column of Franco's Nationalist forces during the Spanish Civil War. The lead vehicle is a German-supplied Panzer I, while the heavily camouflaged second vehicle appears to be a Soviet-built T-26B light tank that has been captured from the Republican forces.

on the road to Vienna. German mobilisation proved chaotic, fuel provision inadequate, and march discipline poor. It was thus fortunate for the Germans that the Austrians failed to resist. Nevertheless, trial and error brought progressive improvement in German mobilisation and deployment during both their October 1938 occupation of the Sudetenland and the March 1939 conquest of the rump Czech state.

By the summer of 1939 the panzer arm had come far. Raised from scratch in just a few short years, it had developed an unrivalled proficiency in the operation of large armoured formations. Indeed, the April 1939 activation of the 10th Panzer Division, though it failed to reach full divisional strength, raised the panzer force to a nominal six armoured divisions by the start of World War II. Serious inadequacies remained, however, the product of Germany's limited resources and continuing internal opposition. The panzer divisions suffered from organisational defects that reflected German inexperience at structuring and operating large-scale armoured forces. In September 1939, the theoretical strength of each German panzer division stood at 592 tanks. Yet dilatory production – particularly of the medium Panzer III and IV tanks – ensured that this establishment was never realised. Even so, the panzer division itself was too 'tank heavy' and lacked supporting arms (initially it fielded only three battalions of motorised riflemen). Another weakness of the pre-war armoured force was its heavy dependence on wheeled motor vehicles. Only about 20 per cent of the vehicles deployed in the panzer divisions were either fully or halftracked, and the rifle infantry sorely lacked an armoured personnel carrier (APC). Indeed, only 68 Sdkfz 251 APCs were in German service at the start of World

Opposite top: *A German officer serving with the Condor Legion in front of a captured Republican T-26B tank supplied by the Soviets. Note the prominent Totenkopf (Death's Head) insignia on his beret.*

Opposite left: *Nationalist crews in an armoured unit formed from Spanish Foreign Legion personnel muster for inspection. The unit is equipped with Soviet-built T-26B light tanks captured from the Republicans.*

Top: *The soldiers of a German Condor Legion unit line up in front of their vehicles for inspection. Behind them are a Kleinerbefehlswagen I (flying the flag), three Panzer I tanks and a motorcycle fitted with a sidecar.*

Above: *A Panzer I tank demonstrates its ability to mount a steep slope in exercises. The flexibility of the track and suspension arrangements is clearly visible as the vehicle reaches the top of this obstacle.*

Above: Three Nationalist officers of the Spanish Foreign Legion wait to inspect forces at an air base. The officer on the left is a colonel, the one in the centre belongs to the armoured corps.

Above: Spanish Nationalist forces with a captured T-26 light tank and a German-supplied Panzer I Model A light tank. The picture offers an opportunity to compare both armoured fighting vehicles, especially the armament. The T-26's 45mm gun gave it a huge advantage in tank-versus-tank combat.

Left: Spanish Nationalist tank crews of the Spanish Foreign Legion's Light Tank Group operate a captured Republican T-26-B light tank. This frontal view shows nicely the substantial 45mm main armament and the large driver's vision port.

War II on 1 September 1939, sufficient to equip only some of the infantry of the 1st Panzer Division. Consequently, lorryborne infantry found it difficult to keep up with the panzer spearheads as the armoured pioneers had originally envisaged.

The growing success and popularity of the armoured force also invited grasping hands. In 1938, the influential cavalry arm raised three light mechanised divisions, and a fourth followed in 1939, each equipped with a tank battalion. The Germans intended these formations to undertake the traditional cavalry missions of reconnaissance and screening, but their existence also served to preserve the cavalry's traditional influence within the German military. Likewise, infantry protests led to both the formation of the 4th and 6th Panzer Brigades earmarked for dedicated infantry support, as well as the motorisation of four infantry divisions. Such initiatives dispersed available tank strength, so that at the outbreak of World War II only 1944 of Germany's 3195 tanks were grouped within its six panzer divisions.

At the onset of hostilities the quality of German tanks also left much to be desired. Germany went to war with an armoured force predominantly equipped with light Panzer I and II training tanks.

Production of the main battle tank, the Panzer III, as well as of the heavy fire-support tank, the Panzer IV, had fallen well behind schedule, and as a result these two tanks comprised a mere 10 per cent of Germany's total tank arsenal. In fact, given the numerous competing demands for Germany's limited resources, only four per cent of German industrial capacity was geared towards tank procurement. Consequently, armour production remained very limited: during September 1939 Germany manufactured only 57 tanks! Nevertheless, the fact that every panzer possessed a radio – unlike those of her enemies – facilitated superior German tactical cooperation that went some way to offset these equipment weaknesses.

The seeds of victory and defeat

Thus the panzer arm that went to war in September 1939 was not the balanced, all-arms, completely mechanised force of which the panzer pioneers had wanted. Germany's limited military resources prevented this, as did Hitler's unwillingness to burden the German people by fully mobilising the nation and economy for war. Moreover, much doubt and scepticism remained concerning what was largely an untried means of war. Considerable armoured resources had also been siphoned off into motorised infantry divisions, light mechanised cavalry divisions and infantry support tank brigades. In addition, the armoured pioneers had failed to conceive the tank as a military instrument that had to be integrated into a realistic inter-service strategy. Indeed, the Nazi state, with its many competing authorities, promoted and fuelled rather than diminished the inter-service

Left: Four Panzer II Model D fast tanks positioned precisely on their transporters. This view illustrates the all-large road wheel arrangement incorporated into this variant, which marked a radical departure from both the preceding and subsequent Panzer II models.

Above: An entire battalion of German armour, spearheaded by Panzer II tanks, manoeuvres in dispersed formation across gently undulating open countryside during pre-war exercises in Germany. On the eve of World War II the German Army possessed six panzer divisions, containing 1944 tanks in total, the majority of them Panzer I and II models.

rivalries inherent in all armed services. Thus little thought and effort had been directed towards coordinating offensive armoured ground warfare with aerial or naval action. The panzer arm that went to war in September 1939, though few recognised it at the time, was therefore an inadequate long-term instrument for success and already contained within it the seeds of its future failure and defeat.

This notwithstanding, the panzer arm still possessed an edge over its enemies in terms of organisation, doctrine and training that would be decisive enough to shatter the balance of power in Europe. Doctrine and training had imbued the German Army with an aggressive offensive verve which encouraged individual initiative. The German successes of 1939–41 owed as much to this audacity as to the qualitative superiority of German tanks or the organisational effectiveness of the panzer divisions.

Britain and France, on the other hand, who together possessed more tanks, many of which were of equal if not superior quality to the panzers, organised their armoured forces primarily for infantry support within a strategic doctrine of defence. Consequently, Anglo-French forces remained untrained either for attack or for fast-paced, mobile action. Germany's early war victories, therefore, were also the product of the strategic, tactical, doctrinal and organisational defects of her enemies. The first German campaign of World War II, its September 1939 invasion of Poland, confirmed beyond doubt the important contribution of enemy weakness to German success.

CHAPTER 2

POLAND, 1939

In September 1939, Nazi Germany's new war machine invaded Poland. The country faced Axis attack from three sides, and not surprisingly proved incapable of halting the German panzers.

Left: A Panzer IV Model C advances during the invasion of Poland. This variant is distinguishable from the Model B by the armoured sleeve fitted to protect the coaxial turret machine gun.

Above: German armour fords a river during the Axis attack on Poland. Engineers have staked out a circuitous route through the shallow water to enable the panzers to cross the obstacle.

The first shots of Hitler's war were fired by the battleship *Schleswig-Holstein* at 0440 hours on 1 September 1939, against Polish positions around Danzig. But the old battleship, dating from 1906, did not set the tone for the campaign. A few minutes later, the Wehrmacht pushed aside the frontier barriers and poured into Poland. The Polish Campaign was the first real test of the new panzer divisions, and the Germans revealed the speed and striking power of these formations to a stunned world when Poland, with its large infantry and cavalry army, fell prey to the German blitzkrieg in only four weeks. At the time, the Allies believed that Poland had been overwhelmed by vast tank fleets and thousands of aircraft, but the reality was different. In fact, the panzer divisions only formed the cutting edge of the German Army, while the mass of the 40 German infantry divisions still had to tramp their way into battle as their forefathers had done – on foot.

Far from the German Army being fully motorised, it fielded just six panzer, four light mechanised and four motorised infantry divisions, plus two infantry support tank brigades and one scratch panzer formation (*Kempf*), and few of these were even at full strength. Some 1900 aircraft in two Luftflotte (Air Fleets)

Left top: A column of Panzer II light tanks advance down a road in Poland in September 1939. In this campaign German armour carried, as their national insignia, a distinctive white cross on the by-now standard field-grey camouflage scheme. This practice fell out of favour during later campaigns when it was discovered that the crosses made excellent aim marks for anti-tank gunners.

Left bottom: A mixed motorised German column advances down a dirt track towards a burning Polish village which has been hit by German artillery. The column comprises motorcycles – including some with sidecars – together with staff and scout cars. The track is typical of the road network encountered by the Germans during the campaign.

Below: Two German Panzer II light tanks pass a solitary infantryman during the advance into Poland. This tank type, equipped with just a 20mm cannon, formed the mainstay of the German Army's tank fleet during the autumn of 1939.

supported these ground troops. Even the panzer divisions were not as powerful as German propaganda boasted, since the Panzer III and IV tanks were still not ready for manufacturing in quantity. The bulk of the 3000-strong armoured force consisted of either the Panzer I, armed with only two machine guns, or the Panzer II, armed with a 20mm (0.8in) cannon; both these tanks were little more than training vehicles. Nonetheless, these mechanised and motorised divisions had an effect far beyond their actual size and strength. The Polish Army consisted of 30 infantry divisions, 11 cavalry brigades with high morale, an obsolete air force of 435 aircraft, but only two armoured brigades with 887 vehicles, most of which were light tankettes.

Thus even before the campaign began the Wehrmacht had the advantage in overall numbers, but the real German advantages lay in the power of her panzer force, the Luftwaffe and the simple but effective plan adopted by the German High Command. Germany had mobilised 98 divisions during August 1939, and concentrated the majority of these forces against Poland. The Germans planned to invade Poland from three main directions: East Prussia, the

Right: German troops stand next to a captured Polish TK or TKS tankette. These two-man armoured scout vehicles normally mounted a 7.92mm Hotchkiss machine gun, although during 1939 a few TKS tankettes were up-gunned with a 20mm NKM cannons.

Below: One of the crew of an eight-wheeled German armoured car caught on film in the middle of stowing baggage on the side of his vehicle. Note the rare, alternative, German national insignia displayed – a black cross with white surrounds – which only became standard after the Polish Campaign.

main German frontier and Slovakia. The German strategy was simple, and drew its inspiration from the traditional German idea of a Kesselschlacht (cauldron or encirclement battle), as developed by Count von Schlieffen from his study of Hannibal's battles.

The German Third and Fourth Armies of Army Group North, under Colonel-General von Bock, were to cut through the Polish Corridor to link East Prussia with the rest of Germany, and to deny the Poles the important port of Danzig. Once the corridor had been forced open, the panzers of General Heinz Guderian's XIX Corps, which consisted of two panzer divisions and two light divisions, would transfer to East Prussia and join the Third Army in its attack towards Warsaw. Guderian had argued convincingly that his panzers should not be tied too closely to the infantry, otherwise their mobility and speed could not be fully exploited. With this plan his corps would play a major part in the campaign. Meanwhile, Army Group South under Colonel-General von Rundstedt, comprising the bulk of German forces in the Eighth, Tenth and Fourteenth Armies, would thrust deep into Poland

Above: Rear view of a column of German Panzer 38(t) tanks. The tactical symbol prominent on the closest vehicle – a yellow 'Y' on the standard field-grey camouflage scheme – identifies this vehicle as part of the 7th Panzer Division.

Top: A column of German armour on the move during the Polish Campaign. The vehicle in the foreground is a Panzerbefehlswagen Model D1 or E – a command variant of the Panzer III. Note the prominent rail antennae on the hull rear for the powerful (20-watt) communications system.

Left: A rear view of two German tanks. The vehicle on the right is a Panzer 38(t), originally constructed for the Czech Army. The tank on the viewer's left, a Panzer I light tank, has been precariously loaded with all sorts of extra equipment.

Right: A column of German tanks parked close to a wide river obstacle. The rear vehicle is a Panzer II, while the three tanks in front of it are Panzer 38(t)s. All are heavily laden with jerrycans filled with extra fuel.

towards Warsaw and Lublin from Silesia, while mounting a subsidiary attack from Slovakia. However, within Army Group South the panzers were dispersed among the various corps and would not operate en masse. This reflected the continued scepticism about the value of the panzer force among many German commanders. These main attacks would be made with great concentration of force on narrow frontages, aiming to burst through the Polish defences quickly and then to surround the main Polish armies. These thrusts were intended to trap the main Polish forces in a giant encirclement west of the River Vistula, overrun Polish mobilisation areas and unhinging Polish defences. Once encircled, the German Army would complete the destruction of its Polish counterpart. Nonetheless, this plan was risky. With the German Army concentrated for the attack on Poland, it meant that the remaining 30 German divisions could only lightly hold their

Below: *A rear view of a mixed German mobile column. The vehicle in front appears to be a Panzerjäger I self-propelled gun. This design mounted a 47mm Czech anti-tank gun in a tall, open shield on top of the Panzer I chassis, which left the vehicle with a narrow and tall silhouette.*

Above: *German troops inspect an abandoned Polish 7TPjw light tank, the most effective armoured vehicle in the Polish Army inventory. Based on the British Vickers E light tank, the 7TPjw mounted a 37mm Bofors gun and featured armour of up to 17mm (0.67in) thick.*

Westwall defences against the French Army of 170 divisions. Hitler, however, was confident that the French would not launch any major offensive in the West while he was occupied in Poland, and events were to prove him right.

Meanwhile, the Poles were caught on the horns of an almost impossible strategic dilemma. With a frontier of 2815km (1750 miles) in length to defend, the Polish Army was stretched thin, and its seven main armies were deployed close to the frontier to cover the mobilisation of reserves and protect vital industries. Once mobilisation was complete, the Polish Army was to mount a fighting retreat to the more defensible line of the Vistula. However, in its effort to defend Poland the High Command had made fatal assumptions based on the Polish experiences of 1920–21, not the reality of 1939. With its divisions spread out and with few reserves, the Polish Army was terribly vulnerable to the new German panzer divisions, which could easily outpace the Polish infantry and cavalry formations in their fighting retreat. Poland was about to become the first victim of the German blitzkrieg.

Above: A mixed column of German scout cars together with a lorry advance down a very muddy lane in Poland. Visible on the lead car's left mudguard is its tactical insignia, painted in white over the standard field-grey paint scheme.

Below: A column of Panzer I tanks drive down a tree-lined road. The second vehicle is the Ladungsleger I. The distinctive structure attached to its rear is a box held by telescopic arms designed to deliver a 75kg (165lb) explosive charge onto concrete defences.

Above: A captured armoured car in German service, parked behind the five-man crew of a 37mm anti-tank gun as they prepare to fire their weapon into the smoke produced from burning buildings. The 3.7cm PaK 35/36 fired a projectile at 760mps (2493fps) up to a maximum range of 7000m (7658 yards).

Even so, this first German attack of World War II took time to build up momentum. When the German offensive began on 1 September 1939, there were numerous instances of nervousness and hesitation among German troops. While the Condor Legion had gained valuable experience in Spain, and the occupation of Austria and Czechoslovakia had also been useful tests for the panzer troops, Poland was their first real taste of combat. Not surprisingly, during the first few days of the campaign many German troops displayed all the signs of untested troops: they were nervous and 'jumpy', sometimes held up by imaginary enemies, or even fired on their comrades. Von Mellenthin records an episode on the first day of the campaign when an aircraft circling a headquarters was fired on by everyone in the vicinity. A Luftwaffe liaison officer in vain tried to stop the firing by explaining that it was a German aircraft, 'a good old Fiesler Storch'. When the aircraft landed, a shaken the Luftwaffe general in charge of close air support stepped out!

Repulse at Mokra

While many German units adapted to combat conditions, they also met with stubborn Polish resistance. The 4th Panzer Division,

operating with the Tenth Army, encountered the stiffest resistance and learnt a hard lesson on 1 September around the village of Mokra. Outnumbered and badly scattered, the Polish *Wolynian* Cavalry Brigade was dismounted and deployed for defence, relying on its meagre complement of Bofors 37mm anti-tank guns and old 75mm field guns to deal with the German panzers. The unsuspecting 4th Panzer Division ran headlong into the Polish defences, and the Poles beat back numerous attacks and inflicted heavy losses. By the afternoon, however, the Germans were pounding the Polish lines with artillery, and combined attacks with infantry and tanks were beginning to make ground. By the end of the day, though, the Poles were still grimly holding their ground, and the 4th Panzer Division had received a severe check from an outnumbered and outgunned opponent, having lost over 30 tanks and many other vehicles. The 3rd Panzer Division, under Guderian's command, also suffered numerous casualties from Polish anti-tank gunners, while the 2nd Motorised Infantry Division's attack bogged down in the face of strong Polish defences.

However, the Polish defenders could not sustain the intensity of the first day of fighting, and once the Germans had got over their initial nervousness their attack was able to progress remorselessly. On 2 September, the German panzers were able to exploit gaps in the overstretched Polish defences and break through the Polish lines, beginning the encirclement of many Polish formations. A young German infantryman noted in his diary at the start of the campaign: 'it is a wonderful feeling, now, to be a German ... The row of tanks has no end. A quarter of an hour, tanks, tanks, tanks.' But the German infantry still had to make forced marches of up to 65km (40 miles) in a day, in the searing dust and heat of the Polish summer, to keep up with the rapidly moving panzer spearheads in front of them. By 3 September, the day on which both Britain and France declared war on Germany, much of the

Polish Army was in retreat, and the German panzers were now driving deep into the Polish rear. The speed and violence of the German assault unbalanced the Poles, who were greatly hampered in their attempt to withdraw and mobilise their reserves. As the Polish armies fell back, they were outpaced by the German armoured spearheads, and as early as 7 September the 4th Panzer Division approached the outskirts of Warsaw. Blitzkrieg had wrecked the Polish plans and doomed most of the Polish Army to encirclement and capture.

Even the undoubted success of the German forces in encircling the Polish armies was not without its problems. As Army Group

Below: A Polish horse-drawn taczanka *(cart) unit after encountering German panzers. Although the Polish Campaign has been portrayed as a clash of modern Nazi technology against dated Polish military capabilities, in reality the German Army remained largely horse-drawn throughout World War II.*

South pushed on towards Warsaw, it left the Polish Poznan Army on its northern flank. Von Rundstedt warned General Blaskowitz, commander of the Eighth Army, to guard his northern flank, but his divisions remained unaware of the threat posed by the Polish forces. In an attempt to staunch the flow of German units towards Warsaw and give the other Polish armies time to retreat to the Vistula Line, the nine Polish infantry divisions and two cavalry brigades of Army Poznan mounted a powerful attack across the Bzura river on 9 September against Blaskowitz's dangerously strung-out 30th and 24th Infantry Divisions. This Polish offensive on the Bzura became the largest single engagement of the war, as eventually 19 German divisions became involved in the fighting. Catching the Germans unprepared, Army Poznan drove the German 30th Division back in rout and inflicted serious casual-

Above: The brutal aftermath of war. A dead body – hands still clasped together – lies on the grassy banks of a river partially covered by a field blanket. German forces suffered comparatively light casualties during the campaign compared to the Polish Army, which lost 66,300 killed.

Top: A German Honour Party raise their standard-issue 7.92mm Karabiner 98k bolt-action rifles into the air ready to fire a salute during the military burial ceremony for one of their fallen comrades. This particular ceremony is in honour of panzer personnel killed in action in Poland.

Above left: A German Kettenrad halftracked vehicle fitted with a 37mm gun advances at the head of a lorried column. At the back of the vehicle can be seen the wheel of the towed trailer, designed to carry additional baggage and stores.

ties. Blaskowitz requested and received substantial reinforcements, which diverted large numbers of German troops from the drive on Warsaw. However, Army Group South did not merely defend against the Polish attack, but also manoeuvred divisions into position to encircle and crush the Polish units. Again, the speed and flexibility of the German panzer force was demonstrated in the ability of the 1st and 4th Panzer Divisions to move quickly to the

Above: A Polish tankette abandoned in the heavily damaged streets of Warsaw. Luftwaffe bombing devastated the city, but the Germans still lost a large number of the tanks they unwisely committed to urban street fighting against determined Polish resistance.

threatened sector and launch a counterattack on the Polish eastern flank. After a week of ferocious fighting, the Polish units were surrounded and exhausted. Mounting a fighting retreat, scattered Polish units managed to escape the German ring and reach Warsaw, but nearly 170,000 Polish soldiers of Army Poznan were forced to surrender.

At the same time, other units in Army Group South had managed to encircle and destroy strong Polish forces around Radom.

By 12 September, 60,000 Polish troops had been captured around this city, and the German panzers had reached Lvov and crossed the River San in the face of retreating Polish units. Meanwhile, the progress of Guderian's XIX Corps had been spectacular and proved the validity of his ideas about the panzer force. After initial resistance in the Polish Corridor, his advance had been so rapid that many of the German infantry divisions marching through the Polish Corridor met with only scant resistance – the panzers had cleared the way. In fact, Guderian's XIX Corps had managed to encircle the bulk of Army Pomorze. With this primary task achieved, on 7 September Guderian moved his corps through East Prussia to the outer wing of the German offensive. He was ordered to drive south beyond Warsaw to prevent any Polish withdrawal. Meeting only limited resistance, his panzers

Above: German infantry and tanks advance together beside a tram line running down a road on the outskirts of Warsaw, as the Nazi noose tightens on the embattled Polish forces still holding out within the city. The 4th Panzer Division suffered heavily in the street fighting in the city.

reached Brest-Litovsk on 15 September, and two days later at Vlodava he linked up with von Kleist's corps which had pushed up from Slovakia , thus completing the double encirclement of the Polish armies.

With these successes, the Polish defence lost all coherence as its armies were increasingly isolated and forced to fight independently against encircling German forces. At the same time, the battle for Warsaw assumed greater importance as a symbol of Polish resistance. As early as the evening of 8 September, the 4th Panzer Division pushed its tanks and armoured cars into the southern suburbs of the city. However, in the narrow streets and facing a well camouflaged and stubborn anti-tank defence, these attacks came to grief and the German tanks became trapped in street fighting. After further attempts the next day, the attacks subsided

as German strength was drawn off by the Bzura counteroffensive. The Germans had discovered the difficulties of using armour in urban areas. By 25 September, the Germans had deployed over 1000 guns and encircled the city with 13 – mainly infantry – divisions. Eventually, on 27 September, after some of the fiercest fighting of the campaign, and at the cost of over 40,000 civilian casualties, General Julius Rommel, the commander of 140,000-strong garrison, surrendered to avoid further unnecessary casualties.

Left: A weary and dishevelled group of Polish prisoners wait to be taken to a German prison camp. All are wearing fatigue caps, of which three are the square-topped design. The soldier in the centre appears incredibly young to be involved in frontline military service.

With the Soviet invasion of eastern Poland on 17 September, the Polish Army was doomed, and many German units had to move back to the demarcation line that was to separate German-held Poland from the new Soviet territories. Indeed, much of the fierce fighting around Lvov had only served to assist the Soviet drive through eastern Poland. Isolated Polish units continued to fight with a courage born of desperation. In the largest tank battle of the campaign, the Warsaw Mechanised Brigade fought against the 2nd Panzer Division around Tomaszow Lubelski on 18 September. By 20 September, this fierce tank battle had ended with the destruction of the Polish armour.

By the end of September only scattered Polish units still remained in the field, but in eastern Poland General Kleeberg continued to fight around Kock and only surrendered on 6 October 1939. With his surrender the Polish campaign was over. On 5 October, when Polish troops were still fighting around Kock, Hitler took the salute of his victorious Wehrmacht in Warsaw, and the Germans could begin to assess the stunning victory they had achieved over Poland.

Polish casualties had been heavy, with 66,300 killed, 133,700 wounded and over 587,000 taken prisoner by the Germans (civilian casualties were greater still). In completing the destruction of

Top: A group of Panzer I tanks line up during an inspection following the end of the successful Polish Campaign. The vehicle with its turret facing backwards highlights the prominent vision slits on both the turret and hull driver's plate. Note also the tactical insignia flags.

Above: A column of German armour advance down a road past impressive Polish civic buildings. The lead vehicle is a Kleiner Panzerbefehlswagen – the command variant of the Panzer I. In this vehicle the turret was replaced by an armoured super-structure which mounted a single machine gun for close defence.

Poland in only four weeks, the Wehrmacht had suffered comparatively light casualties with 16,000 killed and 32,000 wounded. The victory over Poland had not been gained without difficulties, but the Wehrmacht had met and surmounted each challenge. The panzer arm also had learnt important lessons concerning strong anti-tank defences and the difficulties of employing tanks in town fighting. Just as importantly, with 674 tanks destroyed or irreparably damaged during the campaign, the Panzer I and II had finally been proven to be too lightly armed and armoured for use as the main battle tanks. This revelation spurred the employment of the Panzer III and IV tanks – which were to become the backbone of

the panzer divisions in later campaigns. Nevertheless, it was only on 27 September 1939 that the Germans officially adopted the Panzer III for service after 'successful troop trials'. Hitler himself had been presented with the proof of the power of his new panzer arm. When driven past the wreckage of a Polish artillery regiment, Hitler asked Guderian: 'Our dive bombers did that?' When Guderian replied, 'No, our panzers!', Hitler was clearly surprised. Britain and France were also shaken by the demonstration of the Wehrmacht's effectiveness and its new weapons. Unfortunately, these states would enjoy only limited time to absorb the lessons of the Polish Campaign before Hitler turned his panzers upon them.

Above: German cavalry parade before senior officers in October 1939 after the successful capture of Warsaw. Despite their extreme vulnerability to modern firepower, throughout World War II German cavalry continued to be used for reconnaissance and screening duties in certain tactical situations – particularly on the open steppes of the Soviet Union.

Left: German troops pile captured Polish equipment into a square in central Warsaw in early October 1939. Prominent among this cache of mainly small arms are three Bofors 37mm anti-tank guns.

CHAPTER 3
FRANCE, 1940

In just six weeks during May–June 1940, the German panzers decisively defeated numerically superior Allied forces to conquer Holland, Belgium and France.

Left: The French Char B1 bis heavy tank mounted a high-velocity SA 35 47mm gun in the turret, plus a short-barrelled 75mm howitzer in the hull front.

Above: An early variant Panzer IV heavy support tank deployed by one of the 10 panzer divisions that spearheaded the 1940 German onslaught on the West.

When the triumphant German Army marched through Paris on 14 June 1940, it added the final humiliation to an already shocked and defeated French nation. The unprecedented speed with which Germany defeated France in 1940 sent shock waves around the world. A first-rate military power had been completely defeated in just six weeks. However, although the power of the blitzkrieg had been dramatically vindicated, German success in 1940 owed as much to French failings, mistakes and misfortunes as to German military prowess.

In September 1939, the French waited anxiously for the expected blow to come. While the German Army was fully occupied in crushing Poland, Gamelin, the French Commander-in-Chief, launched a minor offensive into the Saarland, but the French did not advance beyond the range of the guns in their Maginot Line forts. After Poland was defeated, the troops returned to the safety of the forts, and both sides settled into what became known as the Phoney War.

As time passed and the Phoney War continued, Gamelin became more confident of French ability to repulse a German

45

Above: A Sdkfz 231 armoured car in the winter of 1939–40. This vehicle, which mounted a 20mm cannon and a coaxial machine gun, was used in the campaigns in Poland and France for scouting and to provide fire support, but after 1940 was relegated to training roles.

Left: General Heinz Guderian observing troops of his XIX Panzer Corps during the 1940 German campaign in the West. Guderian championed German armoured warfare development and in 1937 wrote the influential book, Achtung! Panzer.

attack. By May 1940, the Allies looked to be as strong as the Germans, both in manpower and equipment. The total Anglo-French force, for example, amounted to 2,500,000 men, which was slightly more than the German Army fielded. The Allies also outnumbered the Germans in armour: while the French and British possessed 3500 tanks, the German Army could only muster 2570, and of these almost one-third were Czechoslovakian models. But in the air the Germans outnumbered the Allies by nearly 1000 aircraft, and this superiority was to be critical during the forthcoming campaign. While on paper the Allies looked like a match for the Germans, in terms of morale, training and leadership Hitler's amred forces were in fact far superior. The German Army had gained invaluable experience and a taste for victory in the Polish Campaign – and many of the faults in the panzer divisions had been ironed out.

Above: *A column of six French Hotchkiss H35 tanks advance through fields during the 1940 campaign. The H35 is distinguishable from the almost identical H39 variant by the greater degree of slope to the rear hull decking. The H39 was later used by the Germans in Russia and the Mediterranean.*

Below: *A column of Light Tanks Mark VI A advance with the British Expeditionary Force in France 1940. The Mark VI A mounted one 0.5in and one 0.303in machine gun, and featured an octagonal commander's cupola and two turret smoke dischargers.*

While the French Army continued to rely on doctrine, weapons and tactics more suited to World War I, the German Army was now confident in its new weapons, doctrine and training. More importantly, the German Army's command style was much better suited to the fast-paced nature of armoured warfare. While many members of the German General Staff remained cautious and still did not understand the importance of the new panzer divisions, the widespread use of aufstragtaktik (initiative in command) gave the Germans a tremendous advantage. Aufstragtaktik meant giving a subordinate an overall objective and then leaving him to carry out the mission in his own way. Aggressive panzer commanders like Guderian and Rommel could now lead from the front, using the new power of radio communications to keep in touch with headquarters while retaining the freedom and flexibility they needed to carry out their missions.

Gamelin relied on plans to repel a German invasion of France which had been discussed for many years. The powerful forts of

Top: Towards the end of the German campaign in France, a small number of pre-production examples of the new StuG III assault gun reached the frontline. The StuG III mounted the short-barrelled 7.5cm StuK 37 L/24 gun in a armoured superstructure atop the standard Panzer III chassis.

Above: A column of Panzer III Model Fs on the move along a tree-lined road in France during the 1940 campaign. The commander of each vehicle is precariously positioned out of his turret cupola in order to scan the woods in the valley running along the column's right flank for signs of enemy activity.

Right: A Panzer IV tank deployed in a field in France. In this view the prominent commander's cupola is highly visible, as are the spare track sections fitted to the vehicle's hull front and hull sides. Note also the eight pairs of small road wheels.

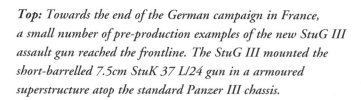

the Maginot Line would defend the French frontier with Germany, while the majority of the French Army's best and most mobile units, along with the British Expeditionary Force (BEF), would be sent into central Belgium to link up with the Belgian Army to fight the decisive battle with Germany on Belgian soil. The French High Command considered that the wooded and hilly terrain of the Ardennes in southern Belgium made it impassable for large enemy formations, and guarded this seemingly quiet sector with the Second and Ninth Armies, both weak and low-grade formations. This deployment would later play straight into Germany's hands.

'Case Yellow'

In fact, the first German plan for an attack on the Western Allies was, if anything, more likely to lead to disaster. After the Wehrmacht had defeated Poland, Hitler, to the astonishment of his generals, ordered an immediate invasion of the Low Countries.

In the short time available his generals prepared an unadventurous plan – codenamed 'Case Yellow' – which envisaged an advance on a broad front into Holland and Belgium, with the main aim of securing the Channel ports for the German Navy. This would not produce the decisive victory that Hitler demanded, particularly since the panzer divisions were not to be used en masse but divided up among the infantry corps. The High Command was not confident of success: some generals believed it might take two years to reach the Channel ports. Even with these obvious flaws, this plan was ordered into action by Hitler no less than 19 times between November 1939 and January 1940. On each occasion his nervous generals were relieved to inform Hitler that the plan had to be postponed due to bad weather. The last cancellation was prompted by the misfortune of a Luftwaffe staff officer. When, on 10 January 1940, this officer, carrying detailed plans for 'Case Yellow', crash-landed in Belgium, the Germans knew that their plan had been compromised. Unfortunately, knowledge of the German

Above: A column of German Panzer II tanks cross a pontoon bridge. The lead vehicle belongs to the regimental headquarters staff, as indicated by the 'R' prefix to the tactical identification number painted on the vehicle's turret sides.

Below: A pair of German soldiers inspect a captured T13 light tank of the Belgian Army. The T13 mounted its light gun in an open-backed, lightly armoured turret, on top of a box-like, riveted hull superstructure.

plan simply reinforced Gamelin's assumption that the Germans would attack through Belgium. Meanwhile, Hitler was now prepared to look at radical new solutions. A minor incident had transformed the whole character of the forthcoming campaign.

Hitler himself had already expressed reservations about 'Case Yellow', and in February he met Major-General von Manstein, Chief of Staff to Rundstedt's Army Group A, who had developed an audacious and imaginative new plan. Army Group B, now with only two panzer divisions but numerous infantry divisions, would invade Holland and northern Belgium, which it was hoped the Allies would mistake for the main attack. Meanwhile, seven panzer divisions, concentrated in Army Group A, would push rapidly through the Ardennes and then cross the River Meuse, the last natural barrier in northern France. Once over the Meuse, the panzers could advance across the plains of northern France at will. By advancing to the Channel coast, Manstein aimed to encircle and destroy the northern Allied armies. This plan offered great results, but was extremely risky because if the Allies detected the advance

through the Ardennes, the long panzer columns could be destroyed by Allied bombers. Nevertheless, Manstein's plan offered Hitler the chance to win the decisive victory he needed.

There had been so many false alarms in the previous months that when the German offensive began on 10 May 1940 at 0440 hours, there was almost a sense of relief within the Allied High Command. This complacent feeling was soon shattered as Army Group B advanced into the Low Countries with unprecedented speed. For the first time in warfare paratroops were used to capture vital points, which split the Dutch defence in two, but the most dramatic of these landings occurred at Fort Eben Emael on the German-Belgian frontier. German glider-borne assault engineers captured this modern fortress, the keystone of Belgium's

Below: A German Panzer 38(t) tank crosses the same pontoon bridge. Originally a Czech design, the 38(t) fielded a 37mm turret cannon plus a coaxial MG 37(t) machine gun, as well as an additional MG 37 in the centre of the hull front.

defence, within a matter of hours. The Luftwaffe also crippled the Allied air effort with a series of pre-emptive strikes against 50 Allied airfields.

Army Group B's spectacular invasion of the Low Countries forced the Allies' reaction, and soon huge columns of Allied troops were pouring into Belgium. Meanwhile, unnoticed by the Allies, the German panzers began to advance into the Ardennes. Using advance parties of engineers and Military Police, the Germans seized vital bridges and road junctions, thus ensuring that the advance through the Ardennes would be swift. Although units of Belgian light infantry and French cavalry put up spirited resistance, they were no match for the panzer divisions who, with plentiful air support, were able to brush them aside and push rapidly on towards the River Meuse. While the French believed that it

Left: A knocked-out British A13 Mark I (Cruiser Mark III) tank of the British Expeditionary Force in France, 1940. This design featured the Christie large road wheel arrangement and mounted a two-pounder gun plus a Vickers 0.303in machine gun.

Right: A German motorised column approaches an abandoned French Somua S35 tank left by the road side. The Somua is distinguishable by the armoured plates protecting the tracks and wheels. The German column includes a signals halftrack, and may well be a headquarters unit.

Below: Two French Hotchkiss tanks – the one in the foreground an H35, the other an H39 – under fire during combat with German forces during the 1940 campaign in the West. The chief difference between these models was the slope to the hull rear.

Above: An extensively damaged French Char 2C heavy tank, probably the victim of German aerial bombing. Constructed during the 1920s, this massive design weighed 69 tonnes (68 tons). The tank mounted a 75mm gun, possessed 45mm- (1.7in-) thick armour, but could manage a top speed of just 19.2km/h (12mph).

would take at least nine days for any force to penetrate the Ardennes, the Germans actually reached the Meuse in only two. The Allies' timetable had been wrecked, and Manstein's bold plan was working.

By late on 12 May, the panzers had reached the Meuse at three points: Dinant, Montherme and Sedan. The main thrust was to be at Sedan, where Guderian's XIX Panzer Corps readied itself for an assault crossing. While the French believed that it would take six days for the Germans to bring up the necessary engineers, heavy artillery and men for an assault crossing, Guderian did not need to wait nearly that long. Since each panzer division had its own integral engineers, artillery, infantry and armour components, and his three panzer divisions (1st, 2nd and 10th) could rely on the Luftwaffe to provide 'flying artillery'

Top: The view from Rommel's armoured command vehicle, as ahead of him the tanks of his 7th Panzer Division cut a swathe of track marks across the long grass of a field in northern France during the 1940 campaign.

Above: Superb view of a Panzer 38(t) in the foreground, advancing across open country with two sister tanks and debussed motorised infantry of Major-General Erwin Rommel's 7th Panzer Division.

Opposite right: The Old and the New – German armour, heavily camouflaged with foliage and concealed near trees in a copse, provide fire support from the rear for a troop of German cavalry as they advance into the open terrain beyond.

for the assault, he was in a position to order his men to cross the river the very next day.

With over 900 aircraft keeping the French defenders' heads down, Guderian's three divisions moved onto the assault. Even though the bank of the Meuse was lined with tanks and guns, which provided heavy direct fire support, French fire was still intense, and the 2nd Panzer Division found it impossible to cross. The 10th Panzer Division also experienced great difficulties, but a small party led by one Staff Sergeant Rubarth managed to effect a bridgehead. At Sedan itself, the 1st Rifle Regiment of the 1st Panzer Division, under the inspirational leadership of Lieutenant-Colonel Balck, breached the French bunker lines and pressed forward over 5km (three miles) from the river. Late in the afternoon, many of the French artillerymen panicked and headed for the rear. Even so, the German bridgehead at Sedan was still precarious – only 5km by 3.5km (three miles long by two miles wide). It was imperative to get German armour across to support the now-exhausted infantry, and so shortly after 2300 hours on 13 May, the engineers of the 1st Panzer Division managed to get a bridge across the Meuse with their last supplies of bridging material. The German gamble of a hasty assault crossing had paid off handsomely.

At Dinant, Rommel's 7th Panzer Division had also met with heavy fire, but with Rommel's personal encouragement the assault succeeded and by the evening his lead elements were across and pushing forward against weakening French resistance. However, at Montherme, Reinhardt's attempt to cross had been thrown back by determined French resistance. Clearly, luck had played its part in the successful German assault crossings but effective tactics had also enabled the Germans to win the upper hand. The aerial bombardment, combined with artillery, tank and anti-aircraft fire had suppressed the French defenders while the infantry and engineers

of the panzer divisions had shown great courage in crossing the Meuse under heavy fire. Motivating the entire force had been the aggressive, inspirational leadership of Guderian and Rommel.

On 14 May, the Allies mounted desperate air attacks, committing a total of 150 bombers and 250 fighters, in an attempt to destroy the bridges at Sedan. But the Luftwaffe flew 800 sorties and Guderian's troops ringed the bridge with 200 anti-aircraft guns. The Allied aircraft were decimated by this heavy defence, and the vital bridges remained intact.

While the planned French counterattacks on 14 May dissolved into uncoordinated piecemeal attacks, Guderian took the bold decision to pivot his corps westwards to make the break-out the next day. With only two-thirds of his corps across the river, and French troops massing to the south of the bridgehead near Stonne, pushing forward without regard to his flanks was a very big gamble on Guderian's part. He managed to persuade his immediate

superior, von Kleist, to agree to the move, but it is certain that had the German High Command known about the full situation it would have ordered a halt.

Although there was fierce fighting on the southern shoulder of the German break-in around the village of Stonne on 15 May, the panzers broke out to the west and Guderian realised that he had cut through the main French defences. By 16 May, Reinhardt had broken out at Montherme and Hoth's panzer corps was fully across the Meuse at Dinant, spearheaded by Rommel's 7th Panzer Division, which was earning the soubriquet 'The Ghost Division' as his men constantly appeared in locations far in advance of where the French expected. That day Guderian's troops linked up with Reinhardt's at Moncornet, tearing a 96km (60-mile) gap in the French line from Dinant to Sedan, and with the panzer divi-

Top: Allied light carriers, based on the Carden-Lloyd tankette chassis, advance along a road in France, May 1940, and pass the wrecked remains of Allied motor vehicles that have been caught by the destructive power of the German Air Force.

Above: Rommel's 7th Panzer Division on the way to the Channel in May 1940. Once away from the Ardennes, the Allies could do little to stop the panzers, though the counterattack by British Matildas at Arras came as a nasty surprise.

Far right: Motorcycles and armoured cars of Rommel's 7th Panzer Division advance down the main street of a French town, and pass the turret-less wreckage of a Panzer III tank. What appears to be the tank's gun barrel is in the middle of the road.

Above: The debris of an army in the aftermath of the Dunkirk evacuation. The British and French forces in the port were saved from destruction at the hands of the panzers by Hitler's famous halt order, though all their heavy equipment was left behind.

sions out into open countryside over 80km (50 miles) from Sedan, there was virtually nothing the French could do to stop them.

The French were not alone in being surprised by the success of the panzer divisions. Hitler, increasingly worried about the vulnerability of the flanks of what was now being called the 'Panzer corridor', ordered a halt on 17 May. For while the panzer divisions now motored across France, much of the German infantry still toiled its way through the Ardennes. Guderian was furious with Kleist, whom he thought was responsible for the order, and in a fit of anger handed in his resignation. It was only the intervention of General List, the Twelfth Army's commander, who saved Guderian. He refused Guderian's resignation and allowed him to carry out a reconnaissance in force. This face-saving formula enabled Guderian to continue his advance across France that night.

As the German break-out gathered pace, the French High Command dissolved into turmoil. Gamelin was sacked and replaced by the even-older General Weygand, which caused a fatal delay in the middle of a critical battle. Gamelin's plans for a major counterstroke on 19 May were shelved by Weygand, and the last real chance the French had to influence the battle had been thrown away.

Even with their enforced halt on 17 May, Guderian's forces reached the Channel coast at Abbeville on 20 May. The Allied northern armies were now caught in a noose between the two German army groups, and these Allied forces were doomed to destruction. However, the next day, 21 May, the most determined Allied counterattack of the campaign took place near Arras. Although the supporting British infantry were held up by Stuka attacks, 60 British Matilda tanks drove straight into Rommel's 7th Panzer Division. As the heavily armoured Matildas lumbered forward, the

Germans realised, to their consternation, that they could not knock out the British tanks with their 37mm anti-tank guns. For a time there was panic among the German troops, and it took Rommel himself to organise a scratch defence line using 88mm anti-aircraft guns to halt the British armour. Although the actual effect of the attack was minimal, as the British were forced to evacuate Arras a few days later, this attack seriously worried the German High Command. Rommel claimed that he had been attacked by three British divisions, and his report gave rise to fears that the Allies might still have powerful forces uncommitted.

In reality, the northern Allied armies were increasingly being forced into a corner, and on 24 May Lord Gort, commander of the BEF, took the decision to evacuate his force from Dunkirk. This was a final admission by the Allies that the destruction of their northern armies was now only a matter of time. However, the BEF was actually saved by a decision taken by Hitler on 23 May. Guderian's panzers were poised to cut off the BEF from the sea, but

Hitler and Rundstedt, worried by the Arras counterattack and concerned about the prospect of fighting in the urban areas of the Channel ports, halted the panzers on the line of the Aa Canal for three precious days, which gave the British and French just enough time to withdraw into a defensive bridgehead around Dunkirk. The Allies managed to evacuate over 338,226 men, including 110,000 French soldiers, from Dunkirk. While this was an astonishing achievement, it could not disguise the enormous disaster which had overtaken the British and the French. While most of the British Army's troops had escaped, almost all of its heavy equipment had to be abandoned, and thus its combat power had been reduced to just rifles and machine guns.

On 28 May the Belgians surrendered, but the battle for France continued. The French had lost their best troops in the disaster in the north, and now had only 49 divisions to hold the Germans along the Somme in the so-called Weygand Line. With Germans now outnumbering the French by two to one, the result was not in doubt. Having rested their troops, the Germans began their second offensive on 5 June, and after two days of heavy fighting shattered the Weygand Line. Now the panzers fanned out across France, driving as fast as they could. The French Government evacuated to Bordeaux, and the Germans occupied Paris on 14 June. Mussolini declared war on France on 10 June, but, much to his shame, the French troops on the Alpine front easily held back the Italian invasion.

A humiliating Armistice was signed between France and Germany on 22 June, and by 25 June all resistance was over. France had been totally defeated in just six weeks. While the German Army was able to enjoy the fruits of victory in Paris for

Above: A rare vehicle in the 1940 German invasion of France, a SiG 33 heavy infantry support gun. This vehicle mounted a short-barrelled 150mm infantry gun in a tall, three-sided, open shield on top of the Panzer I Model B chassis.

Right: A Panzer III Model F with crew parked in a wood in France, May 1940. The two coaxial turret machine guns and the third, hull-mounted one are clearly visible in this picture, as is the internal turret mantlet.

another four years, both the French and Germans had been surprised by the course of events. Even Guderian considered his successful crossing of the Meuse on 13 May 'almost a miracle'. For the French there had been no miracles, only disasters. The Germans, using a bold, risky plan, which threw their massed panzer divisions at a critical point, had wrong-footed their opponents, and using speed, initiative and hard-fighting the panzer commanders – especially Guderian – had never allowed the French the breathing space to recover.

The defeat of France and the collapse of the Western Alliance was a tremendous victory for the German Army in 1940. However, in this triumph lay the seeds of disaster. Hitler became confirmed in his belief that he was an unparalleled military genius, and that his war machine, spearheaded by the panzer divisions, was unstoppable. This conveniently ignored both the risks that had been taken and the luck which had come the Germans' way. After the abortive Battle of Britain, Hitler turned his attention towards the Soviet Union, but the Germans found conditions very different on the steppes of Russia.

CHAPTER 4
NORTH AFRICA

Under Erwin Rommel, the Afrika Korps fought the British for two years in the deserts of North Africa. It achieved stunning successes in numerous battles, but suffered eventual defeat and destruction in Tunisia in early 1943.

Left: A knocked-out Panzer III Mark J, known to the British as the Mark III 'Special', from the 15th Panzer Division in Tunisia, with a dead crewman lying on the running board.

Above: General Erwin Rommel standing in his command halftrack on 21 June 1942, the day he captured of Tobruk. He was promoted to field marshal by Hitler, and became a legend.

When Mussolini declared war on Britain and France on 10 June 1940, he had no idea of the disasters that would overtake the Italian armed forces in his 'parallel' war to Hitler's Blitzkrieg. Yet, by 5 February 1941, the Italian Tenth Army in Libya had been destroyed. British forces had captured 130,000 men and taken Cyrenaica, Libya's eastern province and Tripoli, the capital of the Italian colony, remained virtually unprotected. This Italian disaster forced a reaction from Hitler. The Germans sent Lieutenant-General Erwin Rommel, who had proved himself

in the May 1940 invasion of the West, to Tripoli on 12 February 1941 to command a German force – soon to be known as the Afrika Korps – to bolster its demoralised Italian ally.

Rommel's arrival in Libya signalled the start of two years of warfare in the deserts of North Africa, a campaign which was quite unlike any other theatre of World War II. The troops had to live and fight in the harsh desert conditions, and it was during these hard-fought campaigns that Rommel and his army gained their reputation as masters of armoured warfare. Much of this reputation

Top: British officers conferring beside abandoned Italian M13 tanks at Beda Fomm, where the Italian Tenth Army was destroyed on 4 February 1941, when the British Western Desert Force forced the surrender of 100,000 Italians. This disaster forced Hitler to send troops to shore up the Axis in North Africa.

Above: A British motorised column in Cyrenaica fleeing from an Afrika Korps attack. Rommel and his men, although new to the desert, soon turned the tables on the British, pushing them out of Libya's eastern province in April 1941. This was the beginning of two years of hard desert warfare for both sides.

was based on the exceptional abilities of Rommel himself, who led his Afrika Korps to victory after victory. He was a courageous and daring commander whose unprecedented 'feel' for the battlefield was enhanced by his habit of leading from the front. Rommel also drove his men hard and demanded the highest standards. By leading from the front and sharing the same dangers, as well as the rations, of his men, Rommel gained their unshakeable respect and admiration.

Confident in their leader, the panzer troops of the Afrika Korps also had confidence in their tactics and equipment. While Rommel's forces used Panzer II light tanks for reconnaissance, the heavier Panzer III and IV tanks formed the mainstay of the Afrika Korps. These were tough, reliable medium tanks which were generally better armed and armoured than their British opponents. The Panzer III, with its short-barrelled 50mm gun, and the Panzer IV, with its short-barrelled 75mm gun, could outrange most British tanks. When, during the course of 1942, the Germans up-gunned these tanks with long-barrelled 50mm and 75mm guns, versions the British called the Mark III and IV 'Specials', they outclassed all British tanks until the introduction of the American Grant and Sherman tanks later in the year. The Afrika Korps also possessed powerful anti-tank guns like the 5cm PaK 38, which could knock out most British tanks at 1088m (1000yds). But the weapon which British tank crews really feared was the German 88mm anti-aircraft gun, which could knock out British tanks,

even the heavily armoured Matilda, at 2188m (2000yds). These excellent weapons gave the Germans a distinct advantage in the long-range tank battles fought in the desert, but it was the well practised and sophisticated German tactics which made the Afrika Korps so dangerous. While British tank regiments fought independently, often leaving the British infantry far behind, Rommel's panzer divisions fought as concentrated, all-arms forces.

While the vast expanses of sand and rock constituted a tactician's dream, the vast distances over which the armies travelled turned the fighting into a quartermaster's nightmare. Supply was of crucial importance in the desert, as every drop of fuel, round of

Above: A column of Panzer IIIs moving up to the front. Tank columns moving through the desert generally threw up clouds of choking dust, which made life unpleasant for the crews and concealment almost impossible. Such conditions placed great wear and tear on the engines and tracks of the tanks.

Below: German Panzer IIIs in position around Tobruk in June 1941. The long siege of this port frustrated Rommel and his men. Unable to manoeuvre properly, and confronted by a strong anti-tank defence, the panzers could not break through the British and Australian defences.

ammunition and scrap of food which Rommel's army needed had
to be imported from Italian ports into Tripoli and then transported to the front. This complete dependence on supplies, and the
difficulty of transport in the desert, brought about a see-saw effect
in the fighting. As a victorious army advanced farther from its
bases, it stretched its lines of supply, while the defeated force
retreated back onto its logistical bases, meaning that before long it
could counterattack against the weakened attacker.

When Rommel landed at Tripoli on 12 February 1941, he
immediately began to build up his German force, consisting initially of the 5th Light Division (which was soon transformed into
the 21st Panzer Division). These troops were soon joined by the
15th Panzer Division and, in November 1941, by the 90th Light
Division. These three divisions formed the famous Afrika Korps.
While both the British and German High Commands believed
that it would be months before the Afrika Korps would be strong
enough to mount an offensive, Rommel decided to attack with the
forces he had available. On 31 March 1941, therefore, he mounted an armed reconnaissance at El Agheila, which soon became a
full-scale attack. Shocked by this assault, and hampered by cautious command decisions, the British 2nd Armoured Division did
not counterattack immediately when Rommel's men became
bogged down in a minefield. It was the first of many mistakes
made by British commanders which Rommel exploited ruthlessly.
Instead, he widened his attack and soon the British, over-extended and vulnerable, were in full retreat. The Afrika Korps had
demonstrated dramatically its power and ability in its first campaign.

The German panzers pursued the British across the whole of
Cyrenaica, capturing Benghazi and pushing the enemy all the way
to the Egyptian border, but behind them, the fortress of Tobruk
held firm. With his supply of petrol nearly exhausted, Rommel
had to call a halt. He could not continue his advance into Egypt
while Tobruk held out, and so the Afrika Korps prepared to seize

Above: Crewmen clean the main 20mm armament on their Sdkfz 222 armoured car. These light vehicles played a very important role in the Afrika Korps' reconnaissance regiments. Scouting ahead of the main force, it was their job to find and identify British positions and units in the vastness of the desert.

Left: Given the harsh desert conditions, proper maintenance was essential in keeping the panzer arm up to strength. Here, a mobile workshop's crane has lifted the engine deck off a Panzer III prior to replacing the engine. Both sides always had a large number of their available tank strength in repair.

Right: This is a Panzerbefehlspanzer III Mark E – the command version of the Panzer III. To create more interior space, the main armament was replaced with a dummy gun and the hull machine gun was removed. Note the frame aerial running along the engine deck.

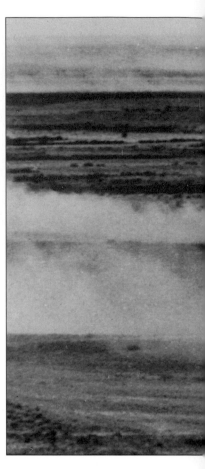

Above: German soldiers dismount from a Horch truck to inspect an Allied dummy 'Honey' tank. This dummy tank may appear crude up close, but from a distance would be indistinguishable from the real thing. Both sides made extensive use of deception to mislead the opposition as to their real strength and intentions.

Above right: German and Italian tanks push across the desert in March 1942. The Afrika Korps had bounced back from its mauling in November 1941, and soon retook Cyrenaica. These tanks are part of the build-up of forces before Rommel launched his outstandingly successful offensive against the Gazala Line.

the fortress in an all-out assault. However, the formidable defences of Tobruk, built by the Italians, improved by the British and tenaciously defended by the 9th Australian Division, came as a considerable surprise to Rommel. The German panzer troops, accustomed to mobile warfare, could not break through the stubborn defence. On 15 August 1941, Rommel was promoted to command the newly constituted Panzer Group Afrika, which comprised the Italian XXI Corps and the Afrika Korps. Meanwhile, the German defence on the Libyan frontier destroyed two hasty British attempts to break the siege, and British tank crews learnt the power of the Afrika Korps in defence. Nonetheless, the Axis forces were unable to breach the Tobruk defences, and as the months passed Rommel became increasingly frustrated.

The stalemate was broken by the British, who launched their newly formed Eighth Army in an attempt to relieve Tobruk on 18 November 1941. Both sides had built up their armoured forces ready for the next round, but while Rommel had amassed 552 tanks, 308 of which were German, the British had superior numbers with 711 tanks. Rommel, still preoccupied with his plans for a further assault on Tobruk, initially ignored the British movements. Thus the Germans were taken by surprise by the British

offensive, codenamed Operation 'Crusader', which swept across the frontier far south of the German defences. The British then held their powerful armoured formations poised ready to fight a climatic battle with Rommel's panzers. But, while the British hesitated around Sidi Rezegh, failing to push on and crush the Afrika Korps, the latter's new commander, General Cruewell, acted. Cruewell concentrated his panzers and fought a series of desperate battles around Sidi Rezegh. Both sides lost heavily, but on 24 November Rommel decided to launch most of the Afrika Korps in a 'dash to the wire' with the hope of forcing the British to retreat. While this dash to the wire did unnerve the British commander, General Cunningham, the gamble failed. General Auchinleck, Commander-in-Chief, Middle East, took over direct command of the Eighth Army and refused to be stampeded by Rommel. Meanwhile, British forces had linked up with the Tobruk garrison and

Right: A Panzer II moves along the coast road in June 1942 towards Mersah Matruh. After the fall of Tobruk, the Afrika Korps advanced into Egypt, hoping for a final victory against the Eighth Army. The coast road, or 'Via Balbia', was of crucial importance for the movement of supplies in the desert war.

Above: A German infantryman inspects part of the defences of Tobruk while the commander of a Panzer II looks on. By 1942, the Panzer II was obsolete, but the Afrika Korps was forced to utilise them due to the chronic shortage of tanks.

Left: A German mobile radio station near Tobruk. Rommel's radio interception unit, under Captain Alfred Seebohm, was adept at 'listening in' to British radio traffic, giving him excellent intelligence about British movements and intentions.

Below: Soldiers look on as Rommel commands the battle for Tobruk in June 1942. Even though he drove his men hard, Rommel's charisma and abilities as a commander inspired great loyalty and affection from his troops.

Rommel was forced to accept that, after sustaining such heavy losses in men and vehicles, he could no longer hold his position around the port. With his supplies running low and the Afrika Korps having lost 340 tanks and 38,000 casualties, Rommel had to take the hard decision to retreat. Grudgingly, and with great skill, the Axis forces retreated all the way through Cyrenaica back to Mersa Brega.

However, Rommel had no intention of staying on the defensive for long. With Malta neutralised by intensive bombing, Axis supply convoys managed to cross the Mediterranean more regularly and Rommel's strength and supplies rapidly grew. On 21 January 1942 Panzer Group Afrika attacked – far sooner than the British had expected. Again the British defence – unprepared and over-stretched – collapsed and within a week the Afrika Korps had

Above: An Eighth Army Sherman tank 'bombing up' before action. The American Sherman, first used at El Alamein in October 1942, gave the British the ability to match any tank in the Afrika Korps' arsenal.

Below: A bivouacked panzer unit. German units often camped on the battlefield itself at night. This gave them an advantage against British armoured forces, who retired to 'laager' away from the fighting. Note the wide dispersal of tents and vehicles to minimise losses during an air attack.

seized much of Cyrenaica back from the British. This time the British stood on the Gazala Line, in front of Tobruk, while both sides built up their forces for another major effort. The British deployment, with the infantry in static defensive 'boxes' and the armour split up to cover the entire line, played into Rommel's hands.

On 26 May 1942 Rommel launched Operation 'Venezia', which would see the virtual destruction of the Eighth Army. His army was now at the peak of its strength with 684 tanks, including 332 German panzers, which compared favourably with the

British total of 849 tanks. The Afrika Korps swept round the southern end of the British line at Bir Hacheim, which was held by a Free French brigade, and motored north on the British side of the minefields, hoping to encircle and destroy the Eighth Army. It was a daring and bold move which revealed the skill of the German panzer troops. The Afrika Korps caught many British armoured brigades by surprise and destroyed them piecemeal. Eventually, British attacks forced Rommel to adopt a defensive position with his back to the British minefields, a position which became known as the 'cauldron'. The Axis position was desperate as the Afrika Korps, starved of supplies, could only hold out for a limited amount of time. Italian engineers worked desperately to gap the British minefields and open a supply route for Rommel's hard-pressed men, to allow them to rebuild their strength. Meanwhile, the German panzer crews and anti-tank gunners decimated the piecemeal British counterattacks.

Rommel takes Tobruk

The final British attempt to crush the 'cauldron' ended in disaster; with the British in disarray, Rommel moved onto the attack. The Afrika Korps dealt with the British defensive infantry 'boxes' one by one, and finally reduced the brave French garrison at Bir Hacheim after an epic struggle. Then, in a hard-fought and confused armoured battle conducted in the desert near the 'Knightsbridge' box on 11–12 June, the Afrika Korps finally broke the power of the British armoured divisions. The Afrika Korps brushed aside the failing British resistance and lunged for Tobruk, and while most of the British forces began to retreat into Egypt, Rommel gave the orders for an assault on the unprepared fortress. This time there was no mistake. Supported by Stuka dive-bombers, the tank and infantry assault delivered by the Afrika Korps overwhelmed the South African defenders of Tobruk who, after a brief resistance, surrendered the port on 21 June 1942. It was Rommel's – and the Afrika Korps' – finest moment.

Some 35,000 British and Commonwealth troops marched into captivity, while the Germans seized 2000 vehicles, 5081 tonnes (5000 tons) of supplies and 1423 tonnes (1400 tons) of fuel to sustain their advance into Egypt. Rommel, now promoted to the rank of field marshal, managed to persuade Hitler to shelve the plans to take Malta in favour of a headlong pursuit of the defeated British. Rommel had his sights set on the glittering prize of Alexandria and Egypt. On 26 June, he bluffed the Eighth Army into retreat at Mersa Matruh and plunged on into Egypt. But the supply situation soon became critical as the Afrika Korps had advanced far beyond its bases. Tripoli was now over 2091km (1300 miles) away, and even Benghazi was 1287km (800 miles) from the front. The ports of Tobruk and Bardia were closer to the front, but were being hammered by RAF bombing. As supplies became scarce, so the strength of the Afrika Korps began to bleed away due to breakdowns, exhaustion and illness.

Below: A rather well used example of a Sdkfz 263 armoured car. This was a special command vehicle for reconnaissance units, which replaced the normal turret with a larger superstructure for extra radios. Panzer crews generally carried much more baggage than normal during desert campaigns.

Above: A group of Italian M13 tanks and Semovente self-propelled guns near Alamein in 1942. The M13s were slow, prone to mechanical trouble and obsolete by 1942, but the crews of the Ariete *and* Littorio *Divisions handled them bravely. Sandbags and tracks supplemented the inadequate armour.*

Below: Italian Semoventes near Alamein in July 1942. The Semovente was based on the M13, but was armed with a 75mm field gun in the hull. They were effective weapons and gave the Italian divisions added firepower. During the fighting at Alamein, they posed real problems for the British infantry.

Opposite top: The panzers retreat. Rommel was forced to withdraw after the damaging and bloody battles fought in the Alamein area. Despite being defeated, the Afrika Korps pulled back skillfully. Note how the commander of this Panzer III is well wrapped up against the cold.

Opposite below: A Panzer III Mark H at speed. Armed with the short-barrelled 50mm gun, it formed the backbone of the Afrika Korps' armoured strength for most of the desert war. A powerful, reliable tank, it outmatched all British tanks until the arrival of the American Grant at the Battle of Gazala in May 1942.

Nonetheless, the Germans pursued the British ruthlessly with their leading tanks and armoured cars, sometimes becoming intermingled with the retreating Eighth Army. On 1 July 1942, the Afrika Korps, without proper reconnaissance, ran into the Alamein Line, and in the face of determined resistance the advance faltered. Unlike any other defensive position in the Western Desert, the El Alamein Line rested on the sea in the north and the Quattara Depression in the south, which meant that the Germans could not outflank the 64km (40-mile) position. Attacks over the next two days also stalled, and Rommel was forced to order a halt. The Afrika Korps was completely exhausted and, with only 37 tanks left, could go no further. Rommel and his panzer divisions were forced to fight a bitter attritional battle against a series of British attacks throughout July 1942. By the end of the month, Rommel feared that his front would crack – there were only 50 Axis tanks in the whole of Africa – but the Axis troops managed to hold on, just. At the end of tenuous supply lines, the panzer divisions could not rebuild their shattered strength quickly enough to restore the situation. As Malta became revitalised, so Allied action against the vulnerable Axis convoys in the Mediterranean increased. Allied attacks sent many vital oil tankers to the bottom, and Rommel's Panzer Army Afrika found itself starved of the fuel it needed to resume mobile warfare.

Nevertheless, by the end of August Rommel felt strong enough to mount one last attempt to break through to the Nile Delta. But although the Afrika Korps swept south around the British minefields, the advance was hampered by lack of fuel, and the panzers could not make the wide hook they needed to encircle the whole of the Eighth Army. Instead, the panzers ran into a tough defen-

sive position on Alam Halfa ridge, and the rebuilt Eighth Army under its new commander, General Montgomery, beat the Germans back after three days of heavy fighting. With the British build-up gathering pace, it was only a matter of time before Montgomery attacked.

On 23 October 1942, the biggest barrage since 1917 announced the opening of the British offensive. This time Montgomery had amassed overwhelming strength. With 1148 tanks at his disposal, he could afford losses which Panzer Army Afrika, with 530 tanks, could not hope to match. Even worse, Rommel was not with his men at this crucial moment. Tired and ill, he had returned to Germany in mid-September and had to rush back when news of the battle reached him. While the German and Italian infantry fought tenaciously, Rommel held back the panzers to counterattack any

Above: A Panzer II accompanies paratroops in Tunisia. Hitler poured troops into the 'Tunisian bridgehead' in the early months of 1943, but Allied control of the air and sea meant the position was untenable – as Rommel had predicted. Hard fighting could not save the Afrika Korps from final defeat and capture.

breakthrough. Slowly, and only after bitter fighting, the British were able to push through the German minefields, and the panzers had to be committed to a desperate battle to seal the breach. Rommel personally led the 90th Light Division in an attack against their old opponents, the 9th Australian Division, but he could not stem the tide.

The end in Africa

After a climatic tank battle at Tel el Aqqaquir on 2 November, overwhelming British strength finally told and the Afrika Korps was shattered. With only 22 tanks left, Rommel knew he must retreat, but Hitler sent a direct order forbidding any withdrawal. It was only the intervention of Field Marshal Kesselring, the Axis Commander-in-Chief in the Mediterranean, that enabled the retreat to continue on 4 November 1942.

While Alamein sounded the death knell for Axis hopes in Egypt, the 'Torch' landings on 8 November by British and American troops in Morocco and Algeria served notice on the entire Axis position in North Africa. Rommel's troops were now facing threats from two sides. The panzer troops, accustomed to victorious advances, now had to get used to long retreats. The Afrika Korps managed to elude every British attempt to destroy it, and fought a series of very effective delaying actions until it paused at Mersa Brega, 804km (500 miles) east of Tripoli, at the end of November 1942. Rommel now realised that the Axis cause was doomed in Africa, but Hitler and Mussolini insisted in sending large numbers of troops to Tunis and Bizerte to hold off the Allied

troops, who had landed after 'Torch'. Hitler appointed Colonel-General von Arnim to command these forces, while Rommel remained in command of his Panzer Army Afrika. This division of responsibility was to lead to fatal confusion in the Axis command.

Rommel pulled out of Libya, abandoning Tripoli which fell to the British on 23 January 1943, and retreated into Tunisia, holding the defences of the Mareth Line against Montgomery's Eighth Army. Meanwhile, von Arnim and Rommel, under the direction of Kesselring, were planning an offensive against the widely spread American forces in western Tunisia. The German commanders were confident that the Tiger, their new heavy tank, would give them a decisive advantage. Tigers first went into action in Tunisia in January 1943. The power of this new German tank was demonstrated on 1 February 1943 along the Rabaa–Pont du Fahs road, when the first Tiger succumbed to Allied fire, but only after it had survived nine previous direct hits from British six-pounder anti-

tank guns! On 14 February 1943, Arnim launched the 10th and 21st Panzer Divisions in an attack designed to take Sidi Bou Zid and split the American positions in two. The panzers, including the 501st Heavy Tank Battalion equipped with Tigers, rolled over the startled American opposition. Panic gripped much of the US II Corps, but von Arnim failed to capitalise on the situation. He refused to release the panzers to Rommel for his attack, and this stalled the Axis offensive while giving the Americans time to regroup. Eventually, on 19 February, Rommel and the veterans of the Afrika Korps attacked into the Kasserine Pass. The Germans overran a number of American positions, but tenacious resistance by isolated groups of American soldiers, combined with tactical mistakes made by commanders more used to fighting in desert than in mountains, meant that the last major attack by the Afrika Korps eventually ground to a halt without inflicting fatal damage on the enemy. The Afrika Korps gave the Americans a painful les-

Above: Bitter defeat. A Panzer III Mark J knocked out at Alamein. Rommel could never get enough of these up-armoured and up-gunned tanks due to supply problems. The grinding 12-day battle in October and November 1942 shattered the Afrika Korps and marked the turning point of the desert war.

son in modern warfare, but failed to cripple them.

On 23 February 1943, Rommel was promoted to overall command in Tunisia but this came too late. The coordination which might have made the Kasserine battle decisive could not save the Axis forces now. Although it fought desperate defensive battles at the Mareth Line and Medenine, the Korps could not turn the tide, and the Allies slowly squeezed the Tunisian bridgehead. On 9 March Rommel left Africa for good, leaving von Arnim to surrender over 250,000 Axis troops to the Allies on the fall of Tunis on 9 May 1943. The panzers had fought their last battle in Africa.

THE EASTERN FRONT, 1941–42

The German panzer force faced its most significant challenge when Hitler unleashed it against the Soviet Union during Operation 'Barbarossa' in summer 1941, a campaign that finally exposed fatal flaws.

Left: A platoon of Panzer III Model H tanks spearheads the German advance across the River Desnja during Operation 'Barbarossa' in June 1941.

Above: German infantry catch a ride on a Panzer III Model G or H tank somewhere in southern Russia during the summer of 1941. Note the mud that clogs the wheels and tracks of the tank.

The spectacular victories the Germans achieved in Scandinavia and France in 1940 proved misleading. Despite its blitzkrieg aura of modernity, the German Army was in many ways less modern than its opponents. Germany was among the least motorised societies in Western Europe: the élite panzer arm remained a small proportion of the army, and Germany lacked the resources to fight a long and protracted conflict. Moreover, what the tremendous victory in the West obscured was that late in the campaign 'friction' had badly eroded the combat power of German mechanised forces. In retrospect, it is clear that blitzkrieg only worked so well early in the war due to a unique combination of German organisational and improvisational skill, the flexibility

Above: A column of Panzer IV Model E tanks passes a convoy of slower-moving soft-skin trucks in Russia during Operation 'Barbarossa', summer 1941. The crew of the leading tank is taking advantage of the continuing good weather to grab some fresh air. The fighting is obviously some way off.

Below: The southern Ukraine, summer 1941. A Panzer II light tank carrying a squad of infantry leads a Sdkfz 251 Model B armoured personnel carrier across a field. In the foreground a squad of infantry advances in single file. At this stage of the campaign the skies were free of enemy aircraft.

Above right: A captured Soviet tankette passes a column of German military vehicles, probably from a reconnaissance unit, parked on the side of the road. In the background an is all-too-familiar sight on the Eastern Front: a column of foot-sore German infantry marching ever deeper into Russia.

Left: A rear view of a column of Panzer III tanks driving through a Russian field. Note the water bottles of the crew hooked on to the rear of the turret, the Swastika flag on the roof to facilitate aerial recognition by German aircraft, and the jerrycans carrying extra fuel on the right-rear mudguard.

instilled by von Seeckt during the interwar era, and the manifest unpreparedness of Germany's enemies.

During the summer of 1940, the German Army absorbed the lessons of the Polish, Scandinavian and French Campaigns. These triumphs confirmed that the panzer force, small as it was, constituted the decisive element in the German Army. This notwithstanding, German tank production continued at a desultory pace during the summer of 1940. Circumstances changed dramatically during July 1940, however, when Hitler unveiled his most grandiose plan to date: the launching of an ideological war of extermination against the Soviet Union, code-named Operation 'Barbarossa'. This operation would be the culmination of the master plan that Hitler had laid out in *Mein Kampf*, the last titanic struggle that would acquire for Germany the 'living space' in the East to guarantee the survival of the Nazi Empire for 1000 years, plus the reduction of the so-called 'sub-human' Slav race to slaves to serve their German masters.

Above: An armoured reconnaissance unit advances through a burning Russian community during the opening stages of Operation 'Barbarossa'. The grenadiers are being transported in light, halftracked artillery tractors interspersed with motorcycle and sidecar combinations.

Opposite above: A captured light tank in German service – note the large cross on the turret side to facilitate identification – advancing past a burning Russian barn. So thinly stretched did German armour become that panzer units had to rely increasingly on captured tanks to bolster their dwindling tank strength.

Right: An early model StuG III assault gun with low-velocity 75mm StuK 37 L/28 gun advancing through a Russian village during September 1941. The immense size of Russia left German armour ever more thinly spread, and increasingly compelled the German Army to utilise assault guns in a mobile anti-tank role.

The proven efficacy of the armoured forces in France and the need for an expanded army for 'Barbarossa' led Hitler to order a massive expansion of mechanised forces during the autumn of 1940, and the number of panzer formations doubled from 10 to 20 divisions. Given the continuing modest production levels, such expansion could only be achieved by halving divisional tank establishments. Historians have traditionally viewed this expansion as a detrimental dilution of the panzer arm. Actually the opposite was true, for the reorganisation, in light of lessons learned in Poland and France, produced sleeker, trimmer and better-organised formations. After-action reports had indicated that the existing divisions were 'tank heavy' and unwieldy. Combat reports also revealed that the panzer division lacked infantry, supporting arms and close integration. Subsequent reorganisation slashed tank strength to a single tank regiment of two or three battalions, with a total tank strength of between 150–200 tanks. The overall result was enhanced combined-arms capabilities and greater fighting power.

The nature and scope of the campaign Hitler envisaged – an ideological and racial war of extermination against the Soviet Union, communism, the Slavs and the Jews – stretched German resources to the limit as her armed forces prepared during the spring of 1941 for the impending campaign. As planning for 'Barbarossa' commenced, Germany stepped up production of the heavier Panzer III and IV tanks, and during the spring of 1941 began to redeploy its forces to the East in preparation for the offensive. Increases in production, however, remained modest as a combination of Nazi arrogance, inflated perceptions of German prowess and traditional German disdain for Russian military capabilities led the Germans to seriously underestimate the resilience and staying power of the Soviet Union. Armour production thus only rose from an average of 182 tanks per month in the last six months of 1940, to an average of 212 in the first six months of 1941.

Operation 'Barbarossa'

Training and exercises during the spring of 1940 brought the panzer arm to a high state of training, leadership and tactics. This was clearly shown in the Balkan diversion that began on 6 April 1941, when five hastily assembled panzer divisions from all over the Reich invaded Yugoslavia and Greece. They achieved an overwhelming victory against a weak enemy woefully deficient in anti-tank capability, but who nevertheless fought in mountainous terrain conducive to defence. During June, these five armoured divisions hastily transferred back to Germany for a brief refit before heading to the East. By 1 June 1941, the German tank arsenal had grown to 5262 tanks, of which 4198 were considered frontline. Hitler committed 17 panzer divisions and 3332 tanks, concentrated in four panzer groups, to 'Barbarossa', the largest assembly of armour in the history of warfare up to that point. But given the vastly greater size of Russia in comparison to France, the German

Below: A column of panzers advance across the open steppe of Russia in dispersed battle formation. The black pall of smoke is a harbinger of battle, and marks a tank that has already fallen victim to enemy fire. The open terrain encountered in much of Russia made for good tank country.

Far left: An early model StuG III assault gun advancing at speed. The number on the front of the vehicle indicates that the vehicle is the third vehicle in the third platoon of an unidentified assault gun battery.

Top right: German troops study with curiosity one of the stranger pieces of ordnance in the Red Army inventory, a wheeled armoured car mounting a heavy anti-tank gun. The open hatches suggest the original crew abandoned the vehicle in a hurry, but it appears intact from the photographer's angle.

Middle right: A German infantry squad rests in and around a slit trench dug behind the protection afforded by a knocked-out Soviet T-34 tank, an armoured fighting vehicle that came as a nasty shock to the Germans during 'Barbarossa'. Note the upturned steel helmet and other kit on the mudguard of the tank, which makes an excellent shelf for refreshments!

Bottom right: A British Mark VI light tank provided under Lend-Lease to the Soviet state. Britain and the United States sent considerable amounts of military hardware to help sustain the Soviet fight against Nazi aggression.

Above: Panzer officers and an NCO examine yet another knocked-out Soviet tank at an unidentified location in Russia during the opening stages of the campaign. In the background, German infantry once again slog their way forward.

Opposite top: A well-camouflaged, heavy artillery piece being towed across a battleground littered with the debris of war. In the foreground, a dead horse and overturned wheel is all that remains of a destroyed horse-drawn limber or carriage. Horses were used in large numbers by the German Army in Russia.

Opposite bottom: A combined-arms armoured spearhead wheels right across a Russian field. Many of the tanks are transporting panzergrenadiers on their hull decks, and several tow the light 3.7cm Pak 35/36 anti-tank gun. Intimate combination between arms of service was one of the key strengths of the German Army.

force/space ratio was actually significantly less than it had been the previous summer. Moreover, of the 3332 tanks deployed, no less than 1156 were obsolete Panzer I and II tanks, originally intended for training, and a further 772 were Panzer 38(t) vehicles of limited combat effectiveness. Therefore, only 1404 Panzer III and IV tanks provided the mainstay of German striking power. Indeed, the German panzer arm now confronted odds far greater than those it had ever faced before, and was both considerably outnumbered and outgunned. For while the Soviet tank inventory contained thousands of obsolete or unserviceable tanks, the Red Army's total armoured strength exceeded 24,000 vehicles. Moreover, unknown to the Germans, the Soviet arsenal included 1475 medium T-34 and KV-1 heavy tanks, superior to any panzer then in German service.

On 21 June 1941, with the benefit of overwhelming surprise, the four panzer groups smashed their way across the border and rapidly

Right: The carnage of war – the bodies of Red Army infantry who had accompanied a tank into the attack lie strewn around the abandoned vehicle. Note the rifle propped up against the rear of the tank, lying where it fell as it dropped out of the lifeless hands of a rifleman.

overwhelmed the Soviet frontier defence forces. The first major tank battle of the campaign took place at Brody on 25 June, between the Fourth Panzer Group and elements of six Soviet mechanised corps, and after a stiff fight ended in a complete German victory. By 3 July 1941, Army Group Centre had completed the elimination of the Bryansk and Minsk Pockets and captured no less than 2585 Soviet tanks. On 10 July, Heinz Guderian's armoured group crossed the Dnepr river near Mogilev, and Smolensk fell six days later. On 5 August, when the last resistance in the Smolensk Pocket ceased, a further 2000 tanks fell into German hands. In the north the Fourth Panzer Group continued its remarkable progress, advancing rapidly through the Baltic states until slowed as Soviet resistance stiffened. On 15 August Novgorod fell, and by the end of the month Leningrad was under siege.

Operation 'Typhoon'

German strength gradually dissipated, however, as Hitler pursued multiple strategic objectives: Leningrad in the north, Moscow in the centre and the economically valuable Ukraine in the south. Moreover, on 19 July Hitler suspended the armoured drive on Moscow and turned Army Group Centre's two panzer groups north and south to assist in the capture of Leningrad and the Ukraine respectively. Historians have interpreted this decision as a crucial strategic error that prevented the capture of Moscow, but even the fall of the Soviet capital probably would not have won the war for the Germans, given the appallingly vicious fighting they had conducted and the absolute nature of their goals. Nevertheless, Hitler's decision paved the way for further enormous victories. On 16 September, Guderian's panzer group driving south met von Kleist's advancing northwards and completed the encirclement of the Soviet Southwest Front in the Kiev Pocket. When the last Soviet resistance ended on 26 September 1941, another 900 tanks had fallen into Germans hands.

The consequence of the Kiev diversion, however, was that Army Group Centre was unable to renew its advance on Moscow until early October 1941, when it launched Operation 'Typhoon'. But by then attrition had inexorably worn down the German armoured spearheads as terrain, topography and the gruelling weather, which varied from sweltering summer heat to deep mud precipitated by autumn rains, inflicted severe losses on German

Top: The speed of the German advance took the Soviets completely by surprise. Here, grenadiers attack burning marshalling yards that contain trains still loaded with newly produced tanks. Never looking a gift horse in the mouth, the Germans probably pressed these particular vehicles into service.

Above: A short-barrelled, early model Panzer IV Model E tank firing at night at the enemy. The Germans preferred not to fight at night if they could avoid it, so perhaps this tank column has encountered one of the more prevalent nocturnal Soviet intelligence-gathering formations.

Right: A Panzer III Model F2 tank platoon enjoying a brief (and no doubt well-earned) respite on the battlefield. The number of the tank in the foreground identifies it as the command vehicle of the fourth platoon of the sixth company of an unidentified panzer regiment.

armour and particularly on soft-skinned wheeled support vehicles. Russia's rivers, primeval swamps and dense forests offered further obstacles to the Nazi advance, behind which the Red Army could bleed the invader. Hitler nevertheless demanded that Moscow be captured before winter, though by October the German Army had suffered heavy casualties and had outstripped its lines of supply. In particular, the strength of the panzer spearheads had diminished rapidly due to non-availability of spare parts, lack of maintenance facilities and the crippling effects of mud and flood. By 1 Septem-

ber, for example, the 17 panzer divisions committed fielded only 1586 operational tanks, only 47 per cent of those that had started the campaign. Contemptuous of Soviet capabilities and possessing an exaggerated faith in German martial prowess, Hitler and the German Army High Command had for too long failed to appreciate the difficulties they faced and the resilience and tenacity of the Soviet defender. In fact, the Red Army offered determined – if frequently amateur – resistance from the beginning. Always first-class fighters, the Soviets quickly learned to become first-class sol-

Above: Russian women and children watch a Panzer III Model G tank advancing down a road. The vehicle passing the tank is a Panzer I Schlepper, a 1939 conversion of the Panzer I tank achieved by removing the turret. Though originally intended as a recovery vehicle, it was too underpowered for such a role.

Left: Two Panzer III Model E tanks parade triumphantly through the streets of an unknown Russian town. A crowd of local inhabitants anxiously observe the Nazi war machine, uncertain about what lies ahead. For many, the future under Nazi rule would be grim indeed.

Below: Young Russian women converse with the crew of a Panzer III tank during Operation 'Barbarossa'. Initially, many non-Russians welcomed the Germans as liberators. Given the grins on the faces of the two cigarette-smoking crew members, one can surmise that the conversation is not about panzer tactics!

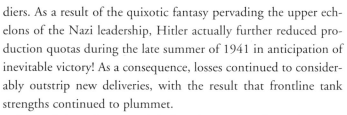

diers. As a result of the quixotic fantasy pervading the upper echelons of the Nazi leadership, Hitler actually further reduced production quotas during the late summer of 1941 in anticipation of inevitable victory! As a consequence, losses continued to considerably outstrip new deliveries, with the result that frontline tank strengths continued to plummet.

Nevertheless, Operation 'Typhoon' experienced initial success. By 20 October 1941, the Germans had surrounded and eliminated Soviet forces at Vyazma and Bryansk, capturing another 1242

Soviet tanks in the process. The heavy, incessant rain that began on 6 October turned the ground into impassable bog and greatly aggravated the mobility and maintenance difficulties of the spearhead German panzer formations, and reduced them to 35 per cent of establishment strength. Thereafter, winter snow started in earnest on 3 November and crippled the final, feeble German push for Moscow initiated on 15 November amid dwindling morale. By this time Guderian's panzer group fielded only 50 operational tanks. One spearhead actually broke into the suburbs of Moscow on 4 December, but was repulsed the next day as the Soviets threw all available troops, including fresh, well-equipped reserves from the Far East, into the line to halt the enemy at the gates of

Left: The Russian terrain proved a major obstacle for the Germans. Here, a motorcycle and sidecar combination has become stuck in soft ground on an ascent. A nearby squad of troops obligingly lend a hand while two Panzer IV tanks wait impatiently to continue the advance.

Bottom left: A short while later – the motorcycle-sidecar combo has gone on its way. Now the Panzer IV tanks can continue their advance. These are the Panzer IV Model D tanks that equipped the panzer platoon of the Grossdeutschland Regiment at the beginning of Operation 'Barbarossa'.

Moscow. The following day, the exhausted, ill-supplied and demoralised German forces, utterly unprepared for winter combat and facing mounting partisan attacks in the rear which further disrupted supply deliveries, assumed the defensive as the German push ground to a halt due to sheer exhaustion. Hitler's gamble on a final big push to take Moscow before winter with tired, depleted and under-supplied forces had failed.

The following day, 6 December, the Soviets enacted a strategic counteroffensive tasked with pushing the Germans back from Moscow on a broad front. The Red Army launched heavy but unsophisticated and ill-coordinated frontal assaults all along the central front in an effort to drive the Germans back from Moscow. This offensive embroiled the depleted panzer divisions that had spearheaded the German advance in heavy defensive fighting. Slow to predict the counteroffensive or to discern its magnitude, the Germans also underestimated their own weaknesses. Inexpert at defence, lacking reserves and dismissive of Soviet capabilities, the Germans conducted inadequate half-measures – piecemeal

Below: A good shot of one of the StuG III Model B assault guns with its short, 28-calibre 75mm gun. Though originally intended to provide infantry fire support, the StuG III actually proved an excellent tank hunter when up-gunned to carry the same L/48 gun as the late model Panzer IV battle tank.

Left: The art of tank maintenance – an excellent shot of the crew of a StuG III Model E assault gun in the middle of replacing a battle-damaged track. This photograph offers a nice view of the idle return wheels on the vehicle, as well as the extra track section mounted on the hull front.

Below: Two Panzerjäger Sdkfz 139 Marder III tank hunters armed with captured 76.2mm Soviet guns on the Eastern Front. The front vehicle illuminates the riveted construction for these improvised tank hunters. The vehicle behind has received a crude winter camouflage – a hastily applied coat of whitewash.

local withdrawals and small-scale unit rotations – that failed to stem the Soviet drive. Forced back in uncoordinated withdrawals, gaps opened in the Wehrmacht lines, through which Soviet forces poured into the Nazi rear. The German front began to disintegrate as the overstretched supply organisation unravelled under the combined effects of winter weather and Soviet dislocation of the German rear. Unused to reverses, German commanders and troops panicked when confronted with their first major defeat of the war.

The Germans faced two strategic options: a major withdrawal to a shorter, defensible winter line (which the generals wanted), or to stand fast and weather the Soviet onslaught, which Hitler chose on 16 December. For once Hitler was right, since a strategic withdrawal in mid-winter with limited mobility, poor serviceability and inadequate supplies would have cost the Germans most of their armour and motor transport, and might well have turned

into a rout similar to Napoleon's retreat from Moscow in 1812. Hitler ordered German forces to stand fast and unflinchingly defend 'hedgehog' positions centred on dispersed fortified village strong points. This 'hold fast' policy, aided by winter weather, ultimately halted the Soviet offensive, as early success led Stalin to launch a general counteroffensive along the entire front between 5 January and late February 1942 that aimed to destroy much of the entire German Army. Only lack of strength and dispersion of effort across the front spared significant German forces from annihilation, however.

The panzer arm in 1942

The German Army never recovered from the horrendous losses of the 1941 campaign. By April 1942, it had lost an incredible 79 per cent of the armour that had began 'Barbarossa', and tank strengths

had plummeted. In addition, massive vehicle losses had significantly reduced mobility. Heavy losses, lack of reinforcement and supplies, as well as undiminished Soviet resistance, also sapped German morale (despite its huge losses in manpower and equipment, the Red Army was still fighting). Both attrition and declining fighting spirit crippled the offensive power of the panzer arm, and curtailed even its defensive capabilities. In retrospect, the 1941 campaign irreparably shattered the panzer arm's striking power.

Left: An armoured reconnaissance unit reconnoitres ahead of the main panzer force with two light, four-wheeled Sdkfz 221 armoured cars. Winter has arrived, and the snow and ice of Russia would have a catastrophic effect on the serviceability of wheeled vehicles like these armoured cars.

Right: A rear view of a Panzerjäger Marder II self-propelled anti-tank gun. An improvised expedient, this vehicle first entered service in the spring of 1942. The Marder II mounted the captured Soviet 76.2mm gun in a lightly armoured, open-topped superstructure on top of the Panzer II Model D or E chassis.

Below: Panzer tanks operating in winter snow during the final push on Moscow. The elaborate white tactical symbol on the rear of the left-hand tank identifies it as belonging the 'Ghost Division' which, under the leadership of Erwin Rommel, had spearheaded the German break-out from the Ardennes in 1940.

Above: A Panzer III Model L tank somewhere in Russia. The tank commander is taking a cautious look at the lie of the land ahead through his binoculars before proceeding. In the background, a truck is bringing up more troops or supplies to the fighting front.

Below: The Russian winter has no favourites. Here, a Russian tank has fallen through the ice and has had to be abandoned. This particular vehicle is a KV-1 heavy tank. At the beginning of 'Barbarossa' in June 1941 the Russians had 500 KVs in service, though a month later only a handful remained in use.

Another contributory factor to Germany's problems was the inferiority of its tanks. Early on during 'Barbarossa', the Germans had been stunned by the ineffectiveness of their tank guns against a hitherto unknown generation of new Soviet medium-heavy tanks. The first German encounter with the Soviet medium T-34 tank occurred during October 1941, when the T-34 badly mauled the 4th Panzer Division at Mtsensk. This finally alerted the German Army to the need for a heavier and more powerful main battle tank to counter Soviet heavy armour. The T-34, in particular, combined mobility, firepower and protection to produce an excellent main battle tank that was superior to any German tank then in service. Examination of captured T-34s quickly ascribed the superiority of the vehicle to three design features absent in existing German tanks: sloped, all-round armour for optimum shot deflection; large road wheels and wide tracks for speed, mobility and stability; and a large-calibre overhanging gun for high muzzle velocity and thus good penetration. Frantic research and development sought to develop a new, third generation of German medium/heavy battle tanks to regain battlefield superiority. In the meantime, the Germans up-armoured and up-gunned existing Panzer III and Panzer IV battle tanks, up-gunned the Sturmgeschütz assault gun for use in an anti-tank role, and improvised a series of light tank destroyers.

Above: *Winter-camouflaged German infantry mount a panzer for a ride. Infantry could not move easily or quickly through winter snow, and so the prospect of a lift on a tank was eagerly accepted. The frozen ground facilitated the movement of armoured units.*

Below: *Panzer IV tanks camouflaged against the winter snow. German armour found itself vulnerable to the Russian winter, and many expedients had to be devised to keep tanks operational. When oil froze in the extreme cold, which it did all too often, crews had to light fires under their tanks just to get them going.*

Above: A motorcycle dispatch rider brings new orders to the crew of a early variant StuG III assault gun advancing amid a cloud of dust somewhere in southern Russia in the summer of 1942.

Above: A German Panzer III Model L tank accompanied by panzergrenadiers resumes the attack again on the central sector of the Eastern Front north of Orel. The squad's two MG 34 light machine guns are to the fore, while the soldier following readies a stick grenade for throwing.

Right: A rear view of a heavy, eight-wheeled Sdkfz 232 armoured signals car. This photograph provides a good view of the large overhanging frame aerial for long-distance communications, which was specifically designed not to interfere with the traverse of the vehicle's 20mm cannon.

In the meantime, the Germans prepared for renewed offensive action during the summer of 1942. Yet the panzer force assembled in June 1942 to spearhead the new offensive in the south – codenamed Operation 'Blue' and designed to capture Stalingrad and the important oil-producing region of the Caucasus – represented a shadow of the force assembled the previous summer. Indeed, a respectable attack force of 10 panzer divisions that fielded 1495 tanks could only be achieved by denuding the rest of the front of armoured support as the Germans went over to strategic defence on the northern and central sectors of the Eastern Front. Of the assembled force, only 133 tanks were the

Above: Panzers advance into action on the Russian Front during the 1942 Summer Campaign, which would lead to the disaster at Stalingrad. The clouds of smoke are testimony to the ferocity of the battle. The tank on the left is towing a light, one-axle trailer carrying drums, no doubt full of extra fuel.

Right: Another Panzer III Model E tank of the Sixth Army cautiously moves down a track somewhere in southern Russia during Operation 'Blue', summer 1942. The accompanying infantry are careful to keep the tank between them and possible danger on their left flank.

latest Panzer IV armed with a long-barrelled 75mm (gun capable of defeating the T-34. Once again, the German plans for the offensive were a jumbled confusion of economic, military and ideological goals. One objective was the attrition and annihilation of Soviet combat forces by large envelopment operations, another was the capture of Stalingrad, yet another was an advance to the Caspian Sea, while finally the Germans envisaged the capture of the oil-producing Caucasus region. In the event, this offensive proved far too ambitious given both the diminution of German offensive strength and the continuing inadequacy of the

supply system, due to the winter hardships and heavy partisan activities in the rear.

However, during the initial stages of Operation 'Blue', launched on 28 June 1942, the Germans met with stunning successes. They quickly tore a 64km (40-mile) gap in Soviet lines, and German forces surged ahead to reach the River Don and burst out into the Caucasus. On 9 August, German mountain troops captured Mount Elbrus, the highest peak in the Caucasus Mountains, and on 2 November the First Panzer Army reached Ordzhonikidze, the most eastern point reached by German forces

Above: A Panzer IV Model F tank advances through a cornfield in the fighting in the sumer of 1942. Behind it, yet another Russian village is left burning. The tank commander wears his headphones in order to maintain constant communication with the driver and gunner.

Opposite top: Another fierce tank battle is in process as fire and smoke obscures much of the forward battle zone. Thus the tank commander has to take the risk of standing up in his turret in order to get a better look of the dangers ahead. What lies ahead is the city of Stalingrad, and the destruction of the Sixth Army.

Right: A German 3.7cm Pak 35/36 anti-tank gun is readied for action. The gunner is about to chamber an armour-piercing round. In the distance in the top left of the picture can just be made out their target – an approaching enemy tank.

during World War II. Though German forces advanced over 965km (600 miles), strategically they had achieved little. In fact, Operation 'Blue' merely served to erode Germany's strategic position in the East, since it greatly extended the Axis front and thinned their forces. Meanwhile, the Soviets conducted a delaying withdrawal that preserved their strength. Greatly extended German lines of communication further exacerbated their already poor logistic system, resulting in growing supply shortages that acted as a brake on continuing operations.

The German advance into the Caucasus was also slowed to a crawl by the increasing diversion of forces to Stalingrad, where a bitter struggle soon developed. Ironically, Stalingrad might have fallen in late July without much of a fight, had not Hitler on the 17th diverted the Fourth Panzer Army south, which delayed the drive on the city by two crucial weeks, during which time the Soviets organised the defence of the urban centre. Consequently, by the third week of August the Sixth Army had been fought to a standstill. Yet Hitler became obsessed with capturing the city named after his arch-enemy, and more and more German forces were sucked into the attritional battle for it, denuding the First

Panzer Army of sufficient strength to conquer the Caucasus. Slowly the German advance came to a halt, with the front stabilising in November. The Red Army seized this opportunity to continue to bleed the Sixth Army at Stalingrad, while husbanding its resources for a strategic counteroffensive against the weak Third and Fourth Romanian Armies deployed on the flanks of General Paulus' command.

On 19 November 1942, the Red Army launched massive offensives to the north and south of Stalingrad, and quickly overran the largely immobile Romanian formations totally lacking in anti-tank capability. The Soviet assault forces rushed forward to link up at Kalach on 23 November 1942 to encircle the German Sixth Army at Stalingrad. Thus within the week the Soviets had achieved what no one had yet achieved in World War II – the encirclement of an entire German field army!

CHAPTER 6

THE EASTERN FRONT, 1943–44

With the abortive German 1943 summer offensive at Kursk, the strategic initiative in the East passed to the Soviets, who subsequently managed to drive the Nazis out of the Soviet Union by late 1944.

Left: A German officer stands in his commander's cupola to scan the horizon. His armband identifies him as belonging to the élite German Army mechanised division Grossdeutschland.

Above: A Hummel heavy self-propelled artillery gun. This vehicle mounted a 15cm sFH 18/1 L/30 howitzer in a lightly armoured, open-topped superstructure on top of the hybrid Panzer III/IV.

When Soviet forces linked up at Kalach and encircled Paulus' Sixth Army at Stalingrad on 23 November 1942, the Germans had little armour in the pocket, as the three encircled panzer divisions had been ground down during the protracted autumn struggle for the city. Short of fuel and munitions and with its mobility hampered by the severe winter weather, the only chance the Sixth Army had was an immediate break-out before the Red Army could consolidate its envelopment. But Hitler forbade the abandonment of Stalingrad, and the Sixth Army soon lost what remaining offensive strength it possessed as the Soviets solidified their siege lines.

Relief could thus only come from the outside, and so Hitler immediately ordered a new offensive to rescue the trapped Sixth Army once XLVIII Panzer Corps had established a new front on

the River Chir. The German counterattack – codenamed 'Winter Storm' – commenced on 12 December, spearheaded by LVII Panzer Corps with three armoured divisions. The German armour advanced 120km (75 miles), but stalled on the Myshkova river on 18 December, some 56km (35 miles) short of the Stalingrad perimeter held by Paulus' beleaguered Sixth Army.

On 16 December 1942, the Soviets renewed their drive west with another massive offensive, designated Operation 'Saturn'. They quickly routed the Italian Eighth Army, and advanced towards Rostov in order to cut off the entire German Army Group A in the Caucasus. Intense Red Army pressure simultaneously pushed back LVII Panzer Corps to its start line by late December, and thus the Sixth Army was doomed. The commander of the newly formed Army Group Don, the gifted Erich von Manstein, fought a desperate delaying defence to allow the First Panzer Army to retreat behind the Don before Rostov fell. At the same time, the Seventeenth Army retreated from the Caucasus Mountains back into

Left: A Nashorn (Rhinoceros) self-propelled anti-tank gun showing the great length of its powerful 8.8cm KwK 43/2 L/71 main armament. To enable the chassis to carry the weight of this weapon, the rest of the vehicle could only be lightly armoured.

Below: Two Nashorn self-propelled guns. The 88mm gun was carried in a lightly armoured superstructure set on top of the hybrid Geschützwagen III/IV chassis. Note the open driver's vision port is open on the vehicle in the foreground.

the Kuban peninsula, which Hitler ordered to be held as a spring-board for a future offensive. However, no sooner had these defensive measures restabilised the front than further disaster struck: the Voronezh Front launched a major assault against the Second Hungarian Army on 15 January 1943. This offensive flung back the Hungarians and led to the recapture of Voronezh on 26 January. Abandoned to its fate, the remnants of the Sixth Army surrendered on 2 February 1943 – 91,000 soldiers went into captivity.

The Germans lost no less than five panzer divisions in the crisis that engulfed them in southern Russia during the winter of 1942–43. For in addition to the three panzers divisions lost at Stalingrad, two others – the 22nd and 27th – were so battered in the bitter defensive struggles on the Don, Chir and Mius rivers that the Germans had to disband them during early 1943. During the spring of 1943, the panzer arm therefore faced a crisis of unprecedented proportions. To date it had lost over 7800 tanks on the Eastern Front, tank strengths had fallen catastrophically, and

Right: Field Marshal Erich von Manstein was unable to rescue the Sixth Army at Stalingrad, but managed to smash the over-extended Soviet spearheads in his Kharkov counteroffensive.

Below: The long-barrelled Panzer IV models remained the spearhead of the German tank corps in the East from mid-1943 to the summer of 1944, and continued to provide sterling defensive work until the end of the war.

Above: An Sdkfz 167 Panzer V Panther command tank – note the antennas for the extra radio equipment the vehicle carried. The location is Russia in the latter stage of the war. Also visible are the vehicle's 90mm smoke dischargers on the turret front. Fatigue is clearly etched on the face of the vehicle commander.

the Soviets had regained the strategic initiative. Indeed, on 23 January 1943 the Germans could muster just 495 operational tanks on the entire Eastern Front!

Hitler recognised the gravity of the situation, and on 17 February 1943 recalled the disgraced Heinz Guderian and appointed him as Inspector General of Armoured Forces, giving him sweeping powers. Guderian's remit was to once again transform the panzer arm into a 'decisive weapon of war'. The new command combined armour, tank destroyers, reconnaissance units, mecha-

nised and motorised infantry and their affiliate training, and replacement units into a new, élite panzer arm that answered to Hitler alone. Guderian set about this task with his customary energy. He demanded, and got, increased production of self-propelled artillery, halftracked armoured personnel carriers (APCs) and anti-tank guns to provide the panzer divisions with both greater mobility and combat power.

After Stalingrad, Hitler finally recognised that Germany was caught in a battle of attrition and ordered total war mobilisation on 22 January 1943. Prodigious efforts during the spring dramatically increased German tank production, so that more tanks were manufactured in the first quarter of 1943 than in the entire second half of 1942. Yet it took time to gear up production and to deliver new vehicles to the front and tank strengths continued to plummet until 1 May 1943, when the German tank inventory reached

a two-year low of 3643 vehicles, of which only 2504 were classified as frontline. Growing shortages compelled the Germans to press a variety of captured British, French and Russian tanks into service – by May no less than 822 foreign tanks were on strength – and to substitute assault guns and tank destroyers for armour. But these measures only partly compensated for the shortage of panzers at the front.

Enter the Tiger and Panther

The introduction into service of two new battle tanks, the Panzer V Panther and the Panzer VI Tiger, accelerated the recovery of the panzer force during 1943. The Tiger, a squat, angular 56-tonne (55.1-ton) heavy tank that mounted a lethal 88mm (3.5in) gun, had its operational debut in August 1942. While heavily armoured and powerfully armed, the Tiger possessed limited mobility and delicate mechanical reliability. Nevertheless, in the hands of an experienced crew and deployed particularly on the defensive, the Tiger was a formidable tank killer. The Panther, developed as a counter to the Soviet T-34, combined a powerful over-hanging 75mm (2.95in) gun and well-sloped armour in a medium-heavy tank, though early vehicles suffered from severe mechanical unreliability. By 1 March 1943, the first 21 Panthers completed had joined 108 Tigers in service alongside the 800 up-gunned Panzer IVs that remained the backbone of the panzer force.

Benefiting from increased production and rationalisation of existing resources, Guderian was able to cobble together a new

Above: In the foreground is a Panzer III Model M produced in early 1943. The new, long-barrelled 5cm L/60 gun and spaced armour increased the battlefield capabilities of the Panzer III, but nonetheless by 1944 the vehicle could not hold its own in combat and was gradually withdrawn to rear-area duties.

strategic armoured reserve which he believed should be utilised exclusively for limited offensive action during 1943, while the panzer arm recovered from its vast winter losses. The first component of that strategic reserve was the new SS panzer corps consisting of the newly upgraded SS Panzergrenadier Divisions *Leibstandarte*, *Das Reich* and *Totenkopf*. During February 1943, Hitler redeployed the SS corps with its 350 tanks to the southern sector of the Eastern Front, where it was skillfully employed by von Manstein in a brilliant master-stroke that rolled back the flank of the Soviet advance into the Ukraine. The commander of I SS Panzer Corps, SS-Obergruppenführer (General) Paul Hausser, disobeyed Hitler's order to hold Kharkov to the last man. Instead he abandoned the city, and from 20 February commenced a series of mobile operations that smashed the overextended Soviet armoured spearheads, flung them back behind the River Donets and recaptured Kharkov on 15 March. In the process the SS panzers destroyed 615 Soviet tanks, but Hausser's fanatics sullied this battlefield success by massacring thousands of Soviet prisoners and civilians as the counteroffensive petered out amid the mud of the spring thaw. Hausser's SS corps had, however, not only driven a

large bulge into the Red Army line centered on Kursk, but had also restabilised the front and brought Germany a desperately needed breathing space.

The success at Kharkov was exactly the kind of economical, limited offensive action that Guderian had envisaged while the panzer arm recovered. Despite all the subsequent efforts, however, the panzer arm was never able to recover from its winter setbacks, as Hitler committed the entire available strategic reserve to a massive strategic offensive, codenamed 'Citadel', which sought to encircle and destroy the Soviet forces in the Kursk salient. 'Citadel' saw further misuse of the panzer arm, for Hitler chose to

meet the enemy on terrain of his own choosing, without the benefit of surprise, against a powerful enemy entrenched in strong fixed defences. Along the two shoulders of the salient the Germans assembled some 17 panzer divisions and two armoured brigades, which fielded between them 2388 tanks for a classic double-pincer encirclement.

In retrospect, Hitler had relied far too heavily on the impact of the new Panther and Tiger tanks for success. To make matters worse, the repeated postponement of the offensive to gain additional tank production cost the Germans the element of surprise. This made it possible for the Soviets to deepen and greatly

Above: A frontal view of a Panzer III Model L with a long-barrelled 5cm L/60 gun. This view shows the additional 20mm- (0.78in-) thick, spaced armour bolted onto the upper hull driver's plate and gun mantlet. Note also the new Kugelblende 50 ball-shaped machine gun mount fitted in the hull, which has been almost hidden by the incorporation of the additional spaced armour.

Above: A Panzer III mounting a 5cm KwK L/42 gun on the Eastern Front in April 1943. Behind it appears to be a Panzer 38(t), few of which were in the frontline by early 1943.

Left: SS-Oberstgruppen-führer (Colonel-General) Paul Hausser, who was nicknamed 'Papa' by the troops under his command. In the spring of 1943, Hausser commanded the newly constituted I SS Panzer Corps which spearheaded Manstein's brilliant Kharkov counter-stroke.

Above: A row of early version Marder III self-propelled anti-tank guns on a production line. This vehicle mounted a 75mm gun in an open-topped, three-sided shield on top of the reliable chassis of the Panzer 38(t) tank.

strengthen their positions, so that the Germans forces ultimately faced by far the most powerful defences they had yet encountered on the Eastern Front. Inevitably, therefore, the battle quickly degenerated into a bitter and savage attritional battle that the Germans could ill-afford and which Guderian had strenuously endeavoured to avoid.

The Panther tank which the Germans had rushed into service for 'Citadel', and of which they expected much, experienced a disastrous debut at Kursk on 5 July, the first day of the offensive. The 250 Panthers committed to 'Citadel' experienced severe reliability problems in combat, due to a combination of frequent breakdowns and engine fires brought about by insufficient ventilation that resulted from watertight sealing of the vehicle for amphibious wading. Widespread damage to gears, transmission and suspension prevented the Panther from living up to expectations, and two days into the offensive only one-fifth of the Panthers committed remained operational. Hitler thus threw away his vital strategic armoured reserve in unsuccessful attrition at Kursk.

Though losses were heavy on both sides, the Germans could not absorb them as readily as the Soviets, and the panzer divisions, laboriously rebuilt by Guderian, were once again burned out.

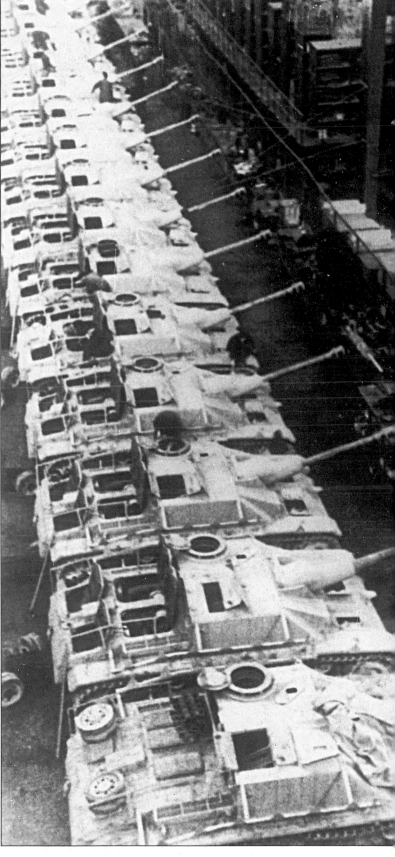

Left: In February 1943, Hitler appointed Colonel-General Heinz Guderian Inspector General of Armoured Troops with sweeping powers to accomplish his remit of rebuilding the power of Germany's depleted panzer arm.

During July, for example, the Germans lost 645 tanks, and in August a further 572 panzers.

The writing on the wall

After Kursk, the German ability to conduct economical mobile defence using mechanised forces to out-manoeuvre and destroy Allied forces – as they had with stunning success at Kharkov – declined as the strategic initiative in the East shifted to the Soviets. From then on the Red Army steadily pushed back the Germans. Alternating constant offensives in different sectors, the Soviets steadily wore down and exhausted the already overstretched German panzer reserves in a prolonged battle of attrition. The panzer divisions became 'fire brigades,' constantly shifting from one crisis point to the next. Though they were still capable of local tactical successes and remained a formidable threat to exposed or ill-supported Soviet forces, they could not reverse Germany's deteriorating strategic position.

Faced with dwindling strength and mobility, the Germans resorted to fortified positional defence. But the Soviet steamroller shattered the Eastern Wall, hastily erected along the Dnepr, during the autumn of 1943, as the Russians sought to recapture the

Above: Mass production of StuG III assault guns. During 1943, with Guderian's encouragement, German AFV production began to rise significantly. One means used to achieve this was to divert industrial capacity away from the construction of tanks to that of assault guns, which were quicker and easier to produce.

Above: A group of Sdkfz 251 mSPW halftracked armoured personnel carriers. These variants are armed forward with either a machine gun or a 37mm cannon. Designed to carry an complete infantry squad, over 16,000 of these vehicles were produced.

Opposite top: As the Germans increasingly needed every available combat-worthy tank at the front, anti-partisan and garrison duties were steadily taken over by a motley assortment of captured enemy tanks like this one.

Opposite below: A side view of a captured Soviet KV-2 heavy tank that shows well the vehicle's monstrously shaped, box-like turret which was designed to house its massive, short-barrelled 152mm howitzer. This tank was not a success.

Right: Excellent view of a German armoured car in Russia. This vehicle is a command variant, with its prominent frame aerial above the turret. German armoured cars were designed so that their tyres could be removed to enable them to run on railway tracks.

Left: German Tiger I tanks being transported by rail up to the frontline prior to Operation 'Citadel' in the summer of 1943. Even with their narrower, transportation tracks these vehicles only just fitted on the standard German railway flat-bed wagon, as can be seen here.

Below: A column of Panzer V Panther tanks being transported by rail for the same offensive. This view illustrates the well-sloped hull frontal armour and the large, interlocking wheel arrangement. At Kursk, though, the Panther would suffer from a number of teething problems.

Ukraine and destroy Army Group South in the process. The Soviet gains isolated the Seventeenth Army in the Caucasus, where it would be smashed during May 1944. Constant attrition prevented substantial expansion of the panzer arm, and thus the German Army never possessed sufficient armoured reserves to counter every enemy breakthrough. Thus when a revitalised Red Army attacked during the winter of 1943–44, it drove Army Group South back to the fringes of the Carpathian Mountains by the spring.

Fighting on the strategic defensive required new tactics and techniques as German armoured forces adapted to new combat realities. Though the tide of battle was against them, the panzers

Above: *Panzergrenadiers snatch a rest close to their Sdkfz 250 leSPW halftracked armoured personnel carrier. This vehicle was smaller than the Sdkfz 251 and could not carry a complete squad.*

Below: *Two Sdkfz 250 light armoured personnel carriers of the Grossdeutschland Division with their respective panzergrenadiers. Each vehicle is armed with a heavy machine gun: the superb 7.92mm MG42.*

Left: German troops next to a StuG III assault gun. The tactical insignia on the vehicle's superstructure side – a yellow helmet – identifies the parent unit as the Grossdeutschland *Division.*

Below: *Excellent side view of a Marder III self-propelled anti-tank gun based upon the chassis of the Panzer 38(t) tank. Behind it is another improvised mid-war German tank destroyer, the Marder II.*

Above: *Crew load 75mm ammunition into their StuG III Model F or G assault gun. Note the vehicle's low silhouette due to its lack of turret – this significantly enhanced its survivability during combat.*

Above: A mixed column of Panzer III tanks advances past a German infantryman at Kursk. The lead tank is a late Model J, retro-fitted with Schürzen turret skirts, while the next two are Model L or M vehicles with extra spaced armour on the hull.

Opposite top: German infantry march across open scrub-land behind a Panzer III tank. The arrangement of small road wheels with return rollers used in early German tank designs contrasted with the large wheels employed in vehicles developed after 1942–43.

could still occasionally achieve stunning local successes that, albeit temporarily, halted the Soviet advance. XLVIII Panzer Corps, for example, conducted a masterful series of mobile engagements during November 1943. The corps counterattacked from Berdichev southwest of Kiev, penetrated 113km (70 miles) into Soviet lines to retake Zhitomir on 18 November, and then encircled the 3rd Guards Tank Army and had annihilated it by 24 November.

However, this was not 1941 and the Soviets rapidly recovered. Faced with mounting enemy strength, in mid-December XLVIII Panzer Corps was forced to retreat and go onto the defen-

sive. On 5 January 1944, the Soviet Second Ukrainian Front launched a new offensive that encircled Kirovgrad. Desperate countermeasures by XLVII Panzer Corps relieved the besieged city, but only at the price of stripping other sectors of the front of units. Consequently, a new Soviet offensive quickly ruptured German defences farther north and encircled 10 divisions, including the 5th SS Panzer Division *Wiking*, in the Cherkassy Pocket on 6 February 1944. III Panzer Corps launched another desperate relief effort, but lacked the strength to reach the trapped troops. Recognising their impending fate, the defenders effected a break-out

on 17 February. In a bloody struggle the survivors battled their way across the freezing Gniloy Tikich stream, leaving all of their heavy weapons behind.

But the successful German escapees leapt out of the frying pan into the fire, for on 24 March Soviet spearheads crossed the Dneistr and the next day encircled much of the First Panzer Army in the Kamenets-Podolsk Pocket east of the river. Hitler dispatched II SS Panzer Corps from France, with the 9th and 10th SS Panzer Divisions, to spearhead a relief effort from Tarnopol, 201km (125 miles) from the beleaguered pocket. A break-out

began on 28 March to coincide with the relief drive, and on 16 April the two forces re-established contact at Buczacz – the First Panzer Army had been saved from destruction.

As stated above, the panzer arm had gradually recovered during 1943, as it began to enjoy the fruits of German total war mobilisation. Tank production soared, and Germany's tank inventory began to rise once more, reaching 5648 vehicles on 1 January 1944 and 6155 on 1 January 1945. The number of heavy tanks also rose steadily, so that by 1 January 1944 there were 373 Tigers and 912 Panthers in service. But despite increasing tank strength, 1944 was to be a dismal year for the panzer force on the Eastern Front. Indeed, the need to despatch ever-increasing numbers of tanks to the Italian and Western theatres prevented any real rise in tank strength in the East. After the Western Allies annihilated the German panzer forces deployed in the West in the summer 1944 Normandy campaign, during the autumn Hitler despatched much of German armoured production to

Right: A view of a sIG 33/1 Model H Bison self-propelled gun. This vehicle featured a 15cm infantry gun in an open-topped fighting compartment mounted on top of the standard Panzer 38(t) chassis. Model M versions featured a superstructure set farther to the rear and the engine at the front.

Above: Close-up detail of the turret and hull front of a Tiger I heavy tank as it rumbles forward at the Battle of Kursk in July 1943. Note set within the hull front plate the well-armoured driver's visor and, on the viewer's left, the Kugelblende 50 ball-shaped machine-gun mount.

Below: A German infantryman lies prone in open grassland while to his right a Panzer III with a long-barrelled 5cm L/60 gun passes by. The Panzer III could be distinguished from the Panzer IV by the fact that it possessed just six pairs of small road wheels rather than the latter's eight.

Left: A Munitionspanzer III. Increasingly from 1943 onwards, many standard Panzer III tanks, when returned to German factories for major repairs, were converted into ammunition carriers by having their turrets removed.

Below: German troops inspect a captured Soviet T-34 tank. This vehicle proved an excellent design, in that it combined the potent firepower of its 76mm gun, the protection afforded by well-sloped armour, and the mobility of large road wheels and wide tracks.

the Western Front, first to stabilise the front and then to rebuild the panzer force for the ambitious December 1944 Ardennes counteroffensive.

Consequently, in the East the dwindling German panzer forces proved unable to stem the Soviet advance into the Reich, and during the second half of 1944 the Germans suffered two more devastating blows in Russia. The first was the complete destruction of Army Group Centre during the great Soviet summer offensive, which saw the annihilation of three panzergrenadier divisions. Soviet armour raced across White Russia into Poland, and the Germans only stopped them with great difficulty on the River Vistula in September, but not before the Red Army was able to establish a bridgehead across the river at Baranov. Try as hard as they might, the German III and XLVIII Panzer Corps proved unable to eliminate the Soviet bridgehead, despite repeated efforts during August and September 1944.

The Soviet First Baltic Front also took advantage of the collapse of Army Group Centre to break through to the Baltic coast and isolate Army Group North in Latvia from the main Axis front. XL Panzer Corps launched immediate countermeasures with four

Below: German tank combat badge, awarded to commanders credited respectively with 75 and 100 'kills' of enemy armour. The panzer ace Michael Wittmann was credited with 120 kills by the time of his death in August 1944.

Above: The crew of a German anti-tank gun prepare to fire at extremely close range at what appears to be a Soviet assault gun approaching out of the smoke. This photograph was probably taken at the Battle of KUrsk.

panzer divisions, and temporarily reopened landward communications with Army Group North on 21 August. No sooner had the central front stabilised in August, however, than a new disaster befell the Germans in the south. On 20 August, the Soviets launched another major offensive against Army Group South which rapidly broke through Romanian forces and precipitated Romania's defection from the Axis alliance five days later, stranding the reconstituted German Sixth Army in Romania – there was seemingly no end to the disasters on the Eastern Front.

Romania's defection also compelled the Germans to enact a difficult and desperate strategic withdrawal from the Balkans. Back in the north, German hopes were dashed further, first by Finland's withdrawal from the Axis war effort, and then by the 10 October Soviet renewal of their offensive against Army Group North, which had isolated the German command in the Courland enclave by the end of the year. On 20 October 1944, the Soviets turned their attentions to Hungary. Here, at the end of the month, German panzer forces achieved their last significant victory on the plains of Debrecen. A series of cut-and-thrust battles fought by the 1st, 23rd and 24th Panzer Divisions isolated and annihilated three Soviet corps. This success provided the Axis with a short-lived respite in Hungary, but by the end of the year continued Soviet advances had encircled Budapest, the Hungarian capital.

The bitter defensive fighting on all theatres badly eroded the combat power of Germany's panzer divisions. Since Germany lacked the resources to simultaneously refurbish so many armoured formations, Hitler ordered the formation of 13 panzer brigades during the late summer, each equipped with a single tank battalion. These were rushed to the Eastern and Western Fronts, but the experiment proved disappointing since the brigades lacked the staying power of panzer divisions, and their inexperience resulted in heavy casualties. During the autumn and winter, the Germans absorbed these brigades into existing divisions in order to rebuild the latter in preparation for the last, great defensive battles Germany's panzers would be called upon to lead in 1945.

Above: Late-model Panzer IV tanks in the winter of 1943–44. Note the eight pairs of small road wheels with four return rollers, and the distinctive Kugelblende 50 hull machine-gun mount.

Right: A bespectacled German officer, with headphones on, looks out from his command cupola on an unidentified German armoured vehicle in late 1943. Note the fur-lined jerkin intended to ward off the chill of the Soviet winter.

Far right: Two of the crew of a German tank or assault gun feed rounds for the vehicle's 7.92mm MG 34 machine gun into ammunition belts. Note the extra wheel and fuel container stowed on the side of the vehicle.

CHAPTER 7

DEFEAT IN THE WEST I: NORMANDY

After its initial failure to throw the Allied D-Day invasion back into the sea, the German Army was decisively defeated in Normandy during the summer of 1944.

Left: American vehicles advance through the remains of a street in St Lo past a knocked-out Tiger I. Allied bombing was so awesome that it left many Normandy towns in complete ruins.

Above: A column of SS Tiger I tanks drive along a road on their way to the Normandy bridgehead. Note the foliage added for camouflage and the extra fuel drums stowed on the hull rear.

Between the autumn of 1943 and June 1944, the previously neglected German Army in the West (the Westheer) worked feverishly to strengthen the Atlantic Wall fortifications along the French and Belgian coasts in order to repel the imminently expected Allied invasion. German uncertainty as to where the Allies would land, plus problems of conflicting command struc-

tures, hampered the Westheer from developing a coherent strategy for repelling the Allied invasion. The overall German Commander-in-Chief in the West (OB West), Field Marshal Gerd von Rundstedt, controlled two army group formations. Army Group G garrisoned southern France, while to the north Field Marshal Rommel commanded Army Group B. Rommel's command comprised

Above: A Panzer IV Model H or J tank of the 2nd Tank Battalion of a German panzer division in Normandy, 1944. Note the large side armour skirting (Schürzen) fitted over the top of the vehicle's tracks to provide protection from anti-tank weapons.

the Fifteenth Army, which controlled the Pas de Calais and the Belgian coast up to the River Scheldt, and Colonel-General Friedrich Dollman's Seventh Army, which defended the coasts of Normandy and Brittany. In addition, von Rundstedt possessed a strategic armoured reserve, Panzer Group West, led by General von Schweppenburg.

The degree of overlapping authority within the German command hierarchy ensured that German plans to repel the Allies remained dogged by disagreement. Rommel's strategy involved holding his mechanised formations as close to the coast as possible, so as to launch a swift counterattack against the Allied invasion when it was most vulnerable. Rommel sought to drive the Allies back into the sea within the first 24 hours of the invasion, since after this time, he believed, the Germans stood little chance of success in the face of the massive strength available to the Allied tactical air forces. However, both von Rundstedt and von Schweppenburg disagreed with Rommel's strategy. They wished to hold back German armour away from the coast to launch a decisive, coordinated counterattack as the Allies advanced from their initial bridgehead. As a solution to these disagreements, Hitler adopted a

compromise strategy that pleased none of the German commanders on the ground.

On the eve of D-Day, the Germans fielded nine panzer divisions – the *Lehr*, 1st SS *Leibstandarte*, 2nd SS *Das Reich*, 2nd, 9th, 11th, 12th SS *Hitlerjugend*, 21st and 116th – plus one panzergrenadier (mechanised) division, the 17th SS. Even though most of these formations remained understrength, overall von Rundstedt's forces still fielded 1500 tanks, including large numbers of Panzer IV and Panther tanks. The Germans deployed the 12th SS and 21st Panzer Divisions in Normandy, the 2nd and 116th Panzer Divisions in the Pas de Calais, and the élite 1st SS Panzer Division *Leibstandarte* in Belgium under the command of SS-Oberstgruppenführer (Colonel-General) Dietrich's I SS Panzer Corps.

Tactical successes

On D-Day, 6 June 1944, the Allied landings in Normandy amid bad weather, caught the Germans by surprise, and consequently the latter's lethargic reaction let slip their best opportunity to drive the Allies back into the sea. During 7–8 June, the SS *Hitlerjugend* and 21st Panzer Divisions attempted to force the British and Canadian troops who had landed before Caen back onto the beaches. While this counter-move failed, German armour managed to foil Allied efforts to increase the depth of their bridgehead. On 7 June, the SS *Hitlerjugend* achieved a notable local success when it repulsed the Canadian drive toward Carpiquet. As the

Above: *A good side view of a Tiger I heavy tank of the 1st Company of an German independent Heavy Tank Battalion standing in front of a typical high-roofed Norman church. Note the finish of the Zimmerit paste on the turret sides.*

Left: *Commander-in-Chief West (OB West), the aristocratic Field Marshal Gerd von Rundstedt, controlled two subordinate Army Group formations plus a strategic armoured reserve commanded by General Gehr von Schweppenburg in Normandy.*

Canadians moved south beyond the villages of Authie and Buron, some 50 Panzer IV tanks hit the exposed Canadian left flank in a well-coordinated counterstroke that flung back the Allied advance.

While the Germans undertook this initial attempt to throw the Allies back into the Channel, they also moved to the bridgehead a new armoured formation, General Bayerlein's Panzer *Lehr* Division, then designated as a Strategic Reserve. During the sunny morning of 7 June, after Hitler belatedly authorised the redeployment of Bayerlein's division, the Panzer *Lehr* commenced its approach march from Alencon. Repeated Allied fighter-bomber attacks ravaged Bayerlein's armoured columns before the *Lehr* even reached the frontline late on 8 June. The next day, I SS Panzer Corps with the *Lehr*, 12th SS and 21st Panzer Divisions, shifted to a defensive posture along a front that ran from southeast of Bayeaux to northeast of Caen. The Germans now altered their

strategy to one of containing the Allied bridgehead until they could rush reinforcements to Normandy. During the last three weeks of June, the Germans redeployed II SS Panzer Corps to France from the Eastern Front for a counteroffensive against the Allied bridgehead. In the interim, the Germans stubbornly defended the terrain north of Caen and St Lo to deny the Allies these key communications centres. During this period another élite German formation, the 2nd SS Panzer Division *Das Reich*, redeployed to Normandy. The division began its move from southern France as early as 8 June 1944, but it did not reach the front until late June, partly thanks to delays inflicted by *Maquis* (French Resistance) attacks. In reprisal for these encounters, SS troops killed 600 unarmed French civilians at Oradour-sur-Glane on 10 June.

Despite the armoured defensive screen the Germans had deployed in front of Caen, on 12 June 1944 the British 7th Armoured Division, the famous 'Desert Rats', nevertheless turned the left flank of the Panzer *Lehr* Division. The next day, as the 'Desert Rats' advanced through the town of Villers Bocage, Ger-

man armour counterattacked. One dozen Tiger tanks from the 101st SS Heavy Tank Battalion, led by SS-Obersturmführer (Lieutenant) Michael Wittmann, smashed the British armoured spearhead. As the tanks of the British 22nd Armoured Brigade advanced towards Hill 213, Wittmann's tanks struck the British force from the rear, and destroyed 29 vehicles in under 15 minutes – the finest feat of armoured warfare witnessed in Normandy. Wittmann's success forced the British to abandon the important penetration they had secured at Villers Bocage, and allowed the Germans to restabilise their positions to the west and north of Caen.

During the last week of June 1944, the German strategy of containment seemed to be working. Panzer Group West's armoured divisions had hemmed in the Allies, and that week the trains carrying SS-Oberstgruppenführer (Colonel-General) Hausser's II Panzer Corps from the East arrived at railheads in France. On the evening of the 28 June, Hausser's Corps, with the 9th SS and 10th SS Panzer Divisions, reached the front around Caen. Four days earlier the Germans had commenced planning for an armoured

Left: A column of Tiger I tanks advance up a winding road towards the Normandy bridgehead. In the lead vehicle, an anti-aircraft 7.92mm machine gun has been fitted to the top of the turret.

Below: A frontal view of a Tiger I heavy tank in Normandy. Extra track sections were usually fitted to the lower hull front and stowed on brackets on the turret sides to augment protection against enemy fire.

Opposite top: A camouflaged four-wheeled armoured car parked on a road in Normandy in early June 1944. The registration plate, prefixed with prominent Waffen-SS runes, distinguishes this vehicle from those deployed by the German Army, which displayed the prefix 'WH'.

Above: The German tank destruction decoration in gold and silver, awarded for a personal effort that destroyed an enemy armoured vehicle. German troops usually employed the Panzerfaust or Panzerschreck anti-tank weapons to gain this award.

Above: A German tank commander supervises the efforts of his crew to camouflage their vehicle with branches and foliage. The vehicle is the lethal Jagdpanzer V Jagdpanther tank destroyer, which mounted a long-barrelled 88mm gun.

Left: Colonel-General Friedrich Dollman, commander of the German Seventh Army. This formation bore the brunt of the Allied landings along the length of the Normandy coast on 6 June 1944.

Far left: A Panzer V Panther medium tank of the 4th Company of an unidentified German armoured division in Normandy. This view highlights the extreme length of the vehicle's potent 7.5cm KwK 42 L/70 gun.

counterstroke by Hausser's Corps that would drive the Allies back into the sea. Allied 'Ultra' intelligence, however, had alerted General Montgomery to the arrival of II SS Panzer Corps. Montgomery realised that he had to resume his offensive to suck German armour into the frontline to prevent Rommel from assembling it in reserve as a counterattack force. So prior to the arrival of Hausser's Corps, Montgomery prepared to launch Operation 'Epsom', an attack by General O'Connor's VIII Corps west of Caen. O'Connor's forces were to advance southeast across the Odon River to capture Hill 112, and then swing east to advance south of Caen. Such an attack would force Rommel to commit his reserve SS armour to forestall the fall of Caen. On 26 June 1944

Left: A small number of King Tiger heavy tanks participated in the later Normandy battles. Most of these vehicles possessed the Porsche turret, with its rounded nose, instead of the standard Henschel production turret.

Right: A member of a King Tiger crew carries out some essential maintenance on the turret front of his vehicle. This picture illustrates the sheer size of the tank's gun mantlet and the rippled effect caused by the addition of Zimmerit anti-magnetic mine paste.

Bottom left: Porsche-turreted King Tigers of an independent German Army unit – the 1st Company, 503rd Heavy Tank Battalion – take cover from the awesome might of the Allied tactical air forces in a wood in Normandy. The other two companies of this battalion were equipped with the Tiger I.

the British commenced 'Epsom', pre-empting the arrival of Hausser's corps by 48 hours. The successful British drive to the Odon forced Rommel to launch the SS armour in a desperate counterattack. Early on 29 June, as Hausser's corps assembled for its attack, the Allies hit it with concentrated artillery and naval gunfire which inflicted severe losses. The SS corps only managed to commence its counterattack the next day, but made little headway over the next three days despite incurring heavy casualties.

Blunting 'Goodwood'

After this failure, Hitler ordered Army Group B to contain the Allies within a narrow bridgehead to deny them the necessary space and terrain to conduct mobile operations. This strategy locked the Germans into an attritional battle in range of Allied naval guns that in the long run they could not win. On 10 July, the Germans withdrew from northern Caen in the face of Montgomery's 'Charnwood' offensive. During the next seven days, Panzer Group West strengthened its defensive positions south of Caen along the vital Bourguebus ridge which dominated the Falaise plain beyond. By 18 July, the Germans had created a powerful, dispersed, defensive belt of considerable depth based on five zones of interlocking strong points. Thus when, on 18 July, Montgomery launched his massive 'Goodwood' offensive, his forces encountered the most formidable German defensive system yet established in Normandy.

In Operation 'Goodwood', the British launched three armoured divisions, one after the other, from their bridgehead east of the Orne to outflank the German positions south of the city. To facilitate their advance, the Allies unleashed a combined artillery and aerial onslaught of unprecedented scale which was intended to obliterate the German defences. The massive Allied bombing and artillery strikes shattered the forward German defences, and initially this enabled the British 11th Armoured Division to advance rapidly. However, the preliminary Allied strikes barely damaged the rearward German defensive positions

on the Bourguebus ridge, which the advancing British troops reached early that afternoon. As the 11th Armoured drove forward, local German armoured reserves launched small counterattacks while they conducted a fighting withdrawal designed to buy time while powerful SS armoured reserves assembled behind the crest of the ridge for a large-scale counter-strike. When launched that evening, the German counterattack all but destroyed the British armoured spearhead in a spectacular battle. Although Montgomery continued his 'Goodwood' offensive until 20 July, the armour of Panzer Group West had effectively halted the momentum of the Allied advance by the night of 18/19 July. Such audacious German use of armour, appropriately combined with the support of other arms, ensured that after 20 July the Bourguebus ridge remained in German hands and a thorn in the side of the Allied forces.

Montgomery had intended 'Goodwood' to draw German armour away from the front around St Lo, to facilitate an American break-out attempt, codenamed Operation 'Cobra'. By the eve of 'Cobra' on 25 July, despite the concentration of German armour under Panzer Group West south of Caen after 'Goodwood', the defences manned by the German Seventh Army at St

Above: British troops shelter close to the bulk of a knocked-out German Tiger I tank. In the foreground can be seen a piece of spare track section attached to the tank's lower hull front, and the boots of a dead German soldier.

Lo remained only slightly weaker than those at Caen. On 26 July, the Americans initiated their 'Cobra' offensive with saturation attacks by Allied strategic bombers, which destroyed what remained of the Panzer *Lehr* Division. During 26–27 July, the Americans easily broke through the German defences and then rapidly exploited this success with deep advances to the south. The main explanation for the unexpected ease of the American advance lay not in Allied tactics nor German force levels, but in the collapsing German logistical system.

The collapse of the Normandy front

During the previous six weeks, the Allies had interdicted to devastating effect the German transportation system in Normandy. In the days prior to 'Cobra', Allied aircraft again knocked out a key rail bridge on the Seventh Army's main supply artery. Consequently, by 26 July German fuel and ammunition stocks in the St Lo sector had sunk perilously low, and these shortages prevented

the still-powerful 2nd SS Panzer Division from employing the mobile counterattack tactics that had proved so successful during 'Goodwood' to stem the American onslaught. Within four days, the Americans had advanced 48km (30 miles) to Avranches, at the foot of the Normandy peninsula, in the face of crumbling German resistance. The American capture of Avranches enabled them to break out of Normandy in all directions into the interior of France. Into this gap in the German line the Americans poured armoured formations of General Patton's newly arrived Third Army. These forces rapidly fanned out to charge west into the Brittany peninsula, south towards the River Loire and east towards Alencon, and beyond that to Paris in the face of minimal German resistance.

Above: A front view of a very heavily camouflaged German Tiger I tank in Normandy in July 1944. Note the anti-aircraft MG 34 fitted to the roof for additional protection against the potent Allied aerial threat. Such measures did not prevent heavy losses to Allied aircraft, though.

As the Americans burst south in 'Cobra' towards Avranches in late July 1944, the British sought, in Operation 'Bluecoat', to widen the 48km- (30-mile-) wide rupture in the German front by attacking south from the Caumont area toward Vire and Vassy. The stretched German forces proved unable to stem the British advance, despite the local successes achieved on 30 July by a dozen newly arrived Jagdpanther tank destroyers. By 8 August, the British had managed to close in on the key town of Vire. Here, the battered Seventh Army achieved one of the last German tactical successes of the Normandy campaign, when SS Tigers destroyed several British tank columns.

During early August 1944, as massed American armour began to fan out in all directions beyond Avranches, Hitler condemned the Westheer to total defeat. The only feasible German strategy was a general retreat back behind the Seine, but instead Hitler ordered Field Marshal von Kluge, the new Commander-in-Chief West, to launch Operation 'Lüttich' from the Mortain area. This

attack involved a powerful armoured counteroffensive by General Hans von Funck's XLVII Panzer Corps. 'Lüttich' aimed to retake Avranches in order to cut off and destroy the 12 American divisions that had broken out to the south. The Germans hastily scraped together the remnants of six mechanised divisions into an armoured strike force that fielded 250 tanks, and built up fuel supplies for a few days of sustained offensive action, though only at the cost of denuding the rest of the front. On the night of 6/7 August 1944, von Funck gained tactical surprise by attacking without a preliminary barrage down the narrow corridor between the See and Selune rivers toward Avranches. However, his forces

Above: *A column of German armour advances towards the Allied bridgehead in Normandy. The rear tank is a Panzer V Panther, with its circular rear turret hatch open. This view clearly illustrates the width of the Panther's tracks, and how vulnerable the column is to air attack.*

Below: *A well-concealed StuG III assault gun in a defensive positions in Normandy in July or August 1944 awaits the next Allied armoured thrust. Note the low silhouette of the vehicle and the Schürzen side armour to ward off attacks by Allied infantry anti-tank weapons.*

Right: An excellent side view of two Porsche-turreted King Tiger tanks that shows the elegant lines of the design and the extreme length of its 8.8cm KwK 43/3 L/71 gun.

Below: A German Tiger I tank stands next to three 7.62cm Feldkanone 288(r) light field guns. This was the German designation for ex-Soviet Pushka obr. 1942g weapons captured on the Eastern Front, and subsequently pressed into service with the Wehrmacht.

proved unable to maintain their advance in the face of the rapid arrival of American reserves. The failure of 'Lüttich' – an operation never likely to succeed – merely drove German armour west, deeper into the noose of a large pocket forming in the Mortain–Argentan area, as the American forces that had broken out at Avranches advanced east to meet up with British and Canadian forces advancing south from the Bourguebus ridge area. Hitler's strategic blunder ensured that in late August large parts of Army Group B would be encircled and destroyed by the Allies.

In early August Montgomery's Canadian forces commenced preparation for Operation 'Totalize', an armoured thrust down the Caen–Falaise road designed to meet up with American breakout forces that now advanced north towards Argentan. The Ger-

mans recognised that if these two thrusts met, much of the Westheer would be encircled, and they therefore maintained powerful defences south of Caen. Massed Canadian armoured columns attacked successfully in darkness during the early hours of 8 August in the wake of heavy bomber strikes. After their rapid penetration of the first German defence line, however, the Canadians paused to allow for another bombing strike before assaulting the second German defensive zone, but this simply gave the battered German defenders time to recover their cohesion. As part of this second phase of 'Totalize', a regimental combined-arms battle group named Worthington Force attempted to seize Hill 195. During the night 8/9, the force became hopelessly lost, and at dawn two small SS armoured battle groups attacked and destroyed

141

Above: An abandoned Tiger I tank in the ruins of a village in Normandy. The insignia on the far side of the hull driver's plate appears to be the crossed-keys of the Leibstandarte, *identifying the parent unit as the 101st SS Heavy Tank Battalion.*

the isolated Canadian force. Indeed, by the evening of 9 August the Germans had successfully utilised their meagre armoured battle groups to halt the momentum of the massed Canadian forces committed to the 'Totalize' offensive. Despite this success, however, it still remained imperative for the Germans to prevent any repeat Canadian attempt to drive south to Falaise to meet up with the Americans at Argentan and hence seal the mouth of the Falaise Pocket. During 14–17 August, these modest German armoured forces again had to conduct a delaying withdrawal in face of a second massed Canadian attempt to capture Falaise, codenamed 'Tractable'.

The Canadians only managed to capture Falaise on 18 August 1944, by which time the remnants of the 20 German divisions threatened with encirclement were withdrawing east out of the Falaise Pocket. Not until 19 August did the Canadian and American advances meet up at Chambois to finally close the neck of the pocket. From outside the pocket the Germans launched a relief effort, spearheaded by the remnants of II SS Panzer Corps. Simultaneously, from inside disorganised German battle groups threw themselves desperately against the blocking positions held tenaciously by the Polish Armoured Division around Trun. Dozens of small German combat teams managed to smash their way out of the pocket, and some 40,000 of the 100,000 encircled German troops managed to escape the 'hell of Falaise'. As these desperate German forces attempt-

Above: Panzer ace SS-Hauptsturmführer (Captain) Michael Wittmann, the driving force behind the bloody repulse inflicted on the 'Desert Rats' at Villers Bocage. He wears the coveted the Knight's Cross with Oakleaf cluster.

Left: A knocked-out Panther tank, a victim of superior Allied firepower in the West in 1944. The vehicle's left turret side armour has been penetrated by Allied fire, and its left track and wheels have been seriously damaged. It is very unlikely that the crew escaped with their lives from the encounter with the enemy.

Below: The wrecked remains of a Panzer III chassis, with part of the rear idler wheel just in view on the right. This chassis probably belonged to a StuG III assault gun, since Panzer III combat tanks were extremely rare in the frontline during the Normandy battles.

ed to break out, the Allies unleashed the full power of their tactical air forces in ceaseless day-time sorties which inflicted terrible damage on German equipment and personnel. By 23 August the Allies had mopped up German resistance in the pocket, and this disaster ensured that Army Group B scarcely retained any cohesion.

German rout in the West

After 21 August, the Westheer degenerated into full-scale retreat as it sought to avoid encirclement in a second, larger, Allied pocket. The Allies now attempted to pin the reeling Germans against the River Seine, over which all the bridges had been destroyed by Allied air attacks. Forced into a hasty retreat during daylight toward the Seine, the Germans suffered heavy losses due to Allied air attack (at this time the British and Americans had complete air superiority over the battlefield, and their fighter-bombers, such as the excellent Typhoon, continually mauled the long columns of German vehicles), while the catastrophic fuel situation forced them to abandon much of their remaining armour.

Between 25–29 August, Army Group B employed every conceivable means to ferry virtually all of its remaining troops over the Seine. In this manner the Germans plucked a success out of the jaws of utter defeat. Once across the Seine, the Westheer continued its disorganised retreat towards the borders of the Reich, as the

Above: German troops in dapple camouflage battledress march down a road next to heavily camouflaged StuG III assault guns in Holland during the autumn of 1944. Note the two stick grenades held by the soldier in the foreground.

Top right: A crew of a Tiger I in the process of repairing the vehicle's right-hand track which it has thrown. Note the mass of extra equipment stowed on the hull rear decking and the fuel cans on the side of the rear hull.

Right: A front view of a 1944-vintage StuG III Model G assault gun fitted with the distinctive rounded lines of a Saukopf (Pig's Head) mantlet. Note also the additional, bolted-on frontal armour around the driver's vision slit.

battle for Normandy came to an end. Overall, during 80 days of bitter combat, the once powerful German Army Group B had lost 1400 armoured fighting vehicles (AFVs) and suffered 600,000 personnel casualties. Reduced, by 31 August, to a strength of 100 AFVs and 200,000 men, all the Germans could do was to retreat in the face of the Allied juggernaut as the latter's forces poured through northern France and Belgium. The Germans were supposedly beaten, though they had one last card to play.

CHAPTER 8

DEFEAT IN THE WEST II: THE ARDENNES

In December 1944 German forces in the West launched a counteroffensive through the lightly defended Ardennes towards Antwerp, which sought to split the Allies in two. But Hitler's last gamble was to prove a dismal failure.

Left: A Tiger I heavy tank undergoing repairs to its track. By the time of the Ardennes counterstroke, the Tiger I was very rare and only a tiny number participated in the operation.

Above: The Germans held a small number of their massive Jagdtiger tank destroyers in reserve during the Ardennes attack and subsequently used them during Operation 'Northwind'.

In early September 1944, as the Allies pushed forward rapidly through Belgium, German armour could do little more that fight delaying actions to cover the retreat of less mobile units. By 10 September, however, the headlong Allied advance stalled due to grossly strained logistics, and this gave the Westheer time to improvise a new defensive crust. To restart Allied forward momen-

tum, the newly promoted Field Marshal Montgomery decided to launch Operation 'Market Garden', an atypically bold operation intended to 'bounce' the River Rhine before the Germans recovered their cohesion. Montgomery ordered General Horrocks' XXX Corps to advance north through Holland and link up with the Allied parachute forces that had landed at key communications

Above: *A pair of Marder III Model M self-propelled anti-tank guns move through a town just prior to the Ardennes Offensive. By late 1944, this vehicle was gradually being superseded in German service by more modern, purpose-designed tank destroyers such as the Jagdpanzer IV.*

Below: *Very few Tiger I heavy tanks participated in the Battle of the Bulge. By this stage of the war the design's thick – but poorly sloped – armour was being challenged by the lethal firepower incorporated into the Allies' newest generation of tank and anti-tank guns.*

Above: The German Assault Tank Battalion 217 deployed eight Sturmpanzer IV Brummbär (Grizzly Bear) assault vehicles during the Ardennes assault. This vehicle mounted a 15cm StuH 43 L/12 howitzer in a heavily armoured superstructure built on top of the standard Panzer IV Model E–G chassis.

nodes along the way. At the northern drop zone, Montgomery ordered the British 1st Airborne Division to seize the bridge at Arnhem and hold it until Horrocks' armour relieved it.

Desperate improvisation by Field Marshal Model, the new commander of the German Army Group B, however, slowed the advance of Horrocks' spearheads. German counterattacks employing Panther and King Tiger tanks threatened the flanks of XXX Corps' advance. Improvised German forces, stiffened by the remnants of II SS Panzer Corps, and reinforced with newly arrived King Tigers, steadily wore down the heroic resistance offered by Colonel Frost's parachute battalion at Arnhem bridge. After six days of resistance, without sign of relief by Horrocks' forces, the German's wiped out Frost's gallant troops at the bridge. Within a few days, further German pressure had also forced the remnants of the entire 1st Airborne Division to withdraw from the Oosterbeek perimeter back behind the Lower Rhine. With these successes, German forces, and in particular their armour, managed to stall the momentum of the Allied offensive in the north.

During the following weeks, the Germans frantically strengthened their fragile defences while the Allies attempted to gain better positions for further offensives. In late October 1944, however, the Germans launched a spoiling attack against the thinly held

Above: Both the squat, angular design of the Tiger I and the massive size of its 8.8cm KwK 36 L/56 main armament are clear from this frontal view of this vehicle accompanied by infantry as the German Army gears itself up for its last great offensive in the West.

positions of General Dempsey's Second British Army in the Peel marshes, southeast of Eindhoven. During the night of 26/27 October, two German mechanised divisions launched a surprise attack in the Meijel area against the American 7th Armoured Division, which had been subordinated to Dempsey's command. Although the Germans gained ground initially, the Allies moved up reinforcements, particularly massed artillery, and then drove the Germans back to their start positions during a 10-day counterattack.

Nevertheless, in the Meijel counterstroke the Germans rudely reminded the Allies that the disasters that they had suffered in Normandy had not entirely extinguished their combat power.

Six weeks before the Meijel counterattack, on 16 September 1944, Hitler had made a momentous decision to launch a larger German counteroffensive that would fundamentally alter the course of the campaign in Northwest Europe. Despite the unfavourable battlefield situation, the Führer nevertheless decided that in the near future the German Army would regain the strategic initiative in the West with a counterblow through the hilly Ardennes region to seize the vital port of Antwerp. On 25 September, Hitler ordered his stunned senior generals to commence planning for such a counteroffensive. During October the Germans produced – under conditions of utmost secrecy – an outline plan for the operation, and then commenced active preparations for the attack, which they earmarked to begin in mid-December 1944.

The Germans allocated Field Marshal Model's Army Group B, with its three subordinate armies, to undertake the counteroffensive. Model spearheaded the offensive with SS-Oberstgruppenführer (Colonel-General) Dietrich's Sixth Panzer Army in the north and General Hasso von Manteuffel's Fifth Panzer Army in the centre; in the south General Brandenburger's Seventh Army, which consisted solely of infantry formations, was to provide flank

Above: A Tiger I heavy tank, vehicle A23, with whitewashed winter camouflage. The tank is parked with its massive gun facing to the right in a snow-covered field on the Western front in December 1944.

Opposite top: A column of King Tiger heavy tanks line up prior to the start of the offensive. These massive vehicles were scarcely suited for the few narrow, winding roads that dissected the hilly, heavily forested terrain of the Ardennes over which the German forces had to fight.

Right: General of Panzer Troops Hasso von Manteuffel commanded the Fifth Panzer Army during the operation.

protection. The Germans decided to attack in the rugged, hilly and heavily wooded terrain of the Ardennes, since its unsuitability for armoured warfare led the Americans to defend this sector with just four divisions. The Ardennes, therefore, despite its unsuitable terrain, nevertheless offered some prospect for limited success because it constituted the weakest part of the Allied frontline. Yet Hitler wanted a strategic, rather than simply a tactical, victory, and insisted that Model's forces advance 153km (95 miles) northwest to seize Antwerp and cut off Montgomery's divisions from the American forces deployed to the south. All the German field commanders involved in the operation, however, insisted in vain that their forces were too weak for such an objective.

The gathering storm

In the six weeks prior to the start of the offensive in mid-December, the Germans undertook a major deception scheme to deceive the Allies as to their intentions. Model's forces employed stringent

security and sophisticated deception techniques to conceal from the Allies the withdrawal from the frontline of the German armour set to spearhead the offensive. During November and early December, the Germans attempted through desperate improvisation to rebuild the seven badly weakened army and Waffen-SS panzer divisions that would lead the counteroffensive.

Two SS armoured corps spearheaded Dietrich's Sixth Panzer Army: SS-Gruppenführer (Lieutenant-General) Preiss' I SS Panzer Corps, with the 1st and 12th SS Panzer Divisions *Leibstandarte* and *Hitlerjugend*; and II SS Panzer Corps, under SS-Gruppenführer (Lieutenant-General) Bittrich, with the 2nd and 9th SS Panzer Divisions *Das Reich* and *Hohenstaufen*. Two armoured corps spearheaded von Manteuffel's Fifth Panzer Army: LVIII Panzer Corps with the 116th Panzer Division, and von Lüttwitz's XXXXVII Panzer Corps with the 2nd and *Lehr* Panzer Divisions. The Germans retained the 21st and the 10th SS *Frundsberg* Panzer Divisions in reserve to exploit any success gained. Overall, the Germans committed approximately 950 armoured fighting vehicles (AFVs), including 52 King Tiger heavy tanks. In the weeks before the offensive, the Germans augmented their infantry strength with 12 newly raised so-called People's Grenadier Divisions, created by throwing together naval and air force personnel, convalescents and Hitler Youth teenagers. To preserve the meagre combat power of the German panzer divisions, Model ordered these People's Grenadier Divisions to conduct the initial break-in operations,

Above: The mobility of the StuG III assault gun made this vehicle highly prized by German commanders during the Ardennes attack. Later models, such as this vehicle, mounted the 7.5cm StuK 40 L/48 gun.

Below: Two Tiger I heavy tanks carry German infantry clothed in white winter over-smocks. The ripple effect caused by the application of Zimmerit anti-magnetic mine paste is clearly visible on both of these vehicles.

Above: German Fallschirmjäger (paratroopers) hitch a ride on an armoured vehicle. The heavily wooded area this group are passing through is indicative of the difficult terrain over which the operation was launched.

and the armour to be committed only for exploitation deep into the Allied rear.

Despite the desperate German efforts to reconstitute the seven army and SS spearhead panzer divisions, on 16 December 1944 they all remained understrength. Instead of fielding the standard two-battalion armoured regiment with about 140 tanks, five divisions possessed just a single organic armoured battalion, with a mixture of about 90 Panzer IV and Panther tanks. To make up for the missing second tank battalion, the High Command allocated to each division a formerly independent assault gun or tank destroyer battalion. Indeed, equipment was so scarce that the 10th SS Panzer Division *Frundsberg* fielded just 10 Panthers, and consequently remained too weak to participate in the offensive. Similarly, the logistical basis for such an ambitious offensive remained utterly inadequate. In particular, the Germans were critically short of fuel, and their plan of attack required that their armour capture Allied fuel dumps in order to continue the offensive. At Hitler's insistence, the Germans gambled everything on the success of a fragile, and scarcely sustainable, surprise blow against the weak spot in the Allied line.

To improve their slim chances of success, the Germans adopted special measures for their counteroffensive. First, acutely aware that Allied aerial superiority hampered enormously their tactical mobility, the Germans decided to counterattack during a predicted period of sustained bad weather that would keep the powerful Allied tactical air forces grounded. They also doubled the number of anti-aircraft tanks deployed in the Ardennes. Second, the Germans undertook two special operations designed to maintain the momentum of their attack. Hitler instructed SS-Standartenführer (Colonel) Otto Skorzeny's 150th Panzer Brigade to sow confusion in the American rear areas in order to facilitate the German advance beyond the River Meuse. Skorzeny's troops, dressed as American Military Police, infiltrated through the frontline to misdirect Allied reinforcements, while German Panthers, cunningly disguised as American M-10 tank destroyers, engaged American forces. The Germans gained only limited tactical advantage from this subterfuge, however, and once Skorzeny's brigade lost the element of surprise it soon suffered heavy casualties. The second special operation involved the drop of 600 paratroopers to seize several key crossroads around Baraque Michel in order to facilitate the advance of the SS *Hitlerjugend* Division.

Above: German troops in Stoumont debate what to do next with captured American soldiers of the 119th Infantry Regiment. One of the German soldiers carries over his left shoulder a Panzerfaust – a disposable personal anti-tank weapon.

Before dawn on 16 December 1944, the Sixth Panzer Army attacked from its positions east of the Elsenborn ridge, and thrust northwest towards the bridges over the River Meuse south of Liege down to Huy. Dietrich first employed his People's Grenadier Divisions to break into the Allied defensive positions before he committed I SS Panzer Corps to develop the German attack into the Allied rear. The German paratrooper drop, however, proved a dismal failure and barely aided the advance of the SS *Hitlerjugend* Division. The parachutists landed dispersed and disorganised, and rapid Allied responses forced them to retreat piecemeal back to the German lines. In addition, the restricted nature of the terrain prevented Dietrich from committing his other armoured force, II SS Panzer Corps, to a second axis of advance. In essence, the thrust developed by the Sixth Panzer Army rested principally on the troops of the SS *Leibstandarte* Division. A reinforced armoured regimental group, the SS Battle Group *Peiper*, spearheaded the advance of the *Leibstandarte*. Led by SS-Obersturmbannführer (Lieutenant-Colonel) Joachim Peiper, the battle group fielded a mix of the relatively mobile Panzer IV and Panther tanks. Peiper had orders to rapidly exploit any success, and to develop the offensive toward Antwerp before the Allies could react.

In the rear of Peiper's forces advanced the attached 501st SS Heavy Tank Battalion, with 30 King Tiger tanks. Thanks to war

Left: General Wilhelm 'Willi' Bittrich commanded II SS Panzer Korps during the Ardennes. His command, which comprised the 2nd and 9th SS Panzer Divisions Das Reich *and* Hohenstaufen, *was initially held back due to constricted lines of communication in favour of Hermann Preiss' I SS Panzer Corps.*

Above: A German mobile column of scout cars and halftracked lorries, both laden with infantrymen, advance along a muddy road in the Ardennes. The towed weapon in the background is a 5cm PaK 38 anti-tank gun.

movies, popular perception associates the Ardennes counteroffensive with this vehicle, but in reality its actual role remained very modest. Peiper's force advanced along a few narrow, winding roads in hilly and heavily wooded terrain, a mission for which the ponderous King Tiger tanks proved particularly unsuited. Peiper wisely placed the King Tigers at the rear of his column, with instructions for them to keep up with the spearhead tanks as best they could, but not surprisingly the heavy tanks soon got left behind.

During 17–19 December, Peiper's armour fought its way forward 40km (25 miles) to Stoumont. However, it was only when Peiper's advance faltered beyond Stoumont on 20 December that 10 of his King Tigers caught up with the lighter spearhead tanks, by which time Peiper's SS fanatics had murdered 77 American prisoners at Malmédy. With Peiper's advance stalled, the Germans desperately needed to open up new axes of advance to maintain the momentum of the offensive. Dietrich entrusted this vital task to the SS *Hitlerjugend* Division, which he ordered to smash the Allied blocking positions at Dom Bütgenbach. The *Hitlerjugend* committed 33 tank destroyers to support the frenzied attacks its fanatical troops made at Dom Bütgenbach. Although this attack proved successful, the SS *Hitlerjugend* subsequently proved unable to restore the momentum of the stalled northern thrust.

Slow German progress

On 21 December, Allied counterattacks surrounded Peiper's troops at La Gleize and cut them off from further logistic re-supply. To make matters worse, on 22 December the mist that had kept Allied fighter-bombers grounded over the previous six days lifted. By the night of 23/24 December, Peiper's force had run out of fuel

and ammunition, and so attempted to exfiltrate out of its encirclement on foot. The force abandoned its remaining 35 tanks, and disabled them to avoid their falling intact into Allied hands. With the destruction of Peiper's force went the demise of the drive of I SS Panzer Corps. Only now, on 22 December, once Peiper's advance had stalled, did Dietrich commit II SS Corps in an attempt to rescue the stalled northern thrust. Its attack also soon met with failure. By Boxing Day, the northern thrust developed by the SS-dominated Sixth Panzer Army, which enjoyed more luxurious equipment levels than Fifth Panzer Army, had proved to be a dismal and costly failure.

Progress of the Fifth Panzer Army

During the first hours of the Ardennes counteroffensive, to the south of Sixth Panzer Army, General Manteuffel's Fifth Panzer Army also advanced after dawn on 16 December. Staunch American resistance around St Vith successfully held the infantry attacks launched in the north of Manteuffel's sector. Farther to the south, however, his two panzer corps successfully thrust 32km (20 miles) towards Houffalize and Bastogne during the first 48 hours. Late on 18 December, as the Panzer *Lehr* approached Bastogne, the 2nd Panzer Division bypassed the town and continued its advance west towards the Meuse bridges around Dinant. During the following day, the 116th Panzer Division captured the key village of

Left: A Tiger I in winter camouflage. This design was too wide for the Germans to carry on their standard railway flat-bed wagon and so was designed with an ingenious two-set track arrangement – with narrow tracks for transportation and wider ones for combat.

Below: Two German infantry-men hold a conversation next to a knocked-out American tank destroyer. On the right, an eight-wheeled heavy armoured car negotiates the uneven ground. The star antennae on the vehicle's rear right identifies it as a command variant.

Right: Lieutenant-Colonel Joachim Peiper, commander of Kampfgruppe *Peiper, spearhead of the 1st SS Panzer Division. The Allies sentenced Peiper to death for his role in the Malmédy massacre, though this was later commuted to life imprisonment.*

Below: German troops stand next to a Tiger I heavy tank covered in rough winter whitewash. The interlocking wheel arrangement and the extra track parts stowed on the turret sides can be seen clearly in this picture.

Houffalize. By 22 December, the Germans had completely surrounded the American garrison at Bastogne, while the next day the 2nd Panzer Division advanced to just 6km (four miles) short of the Meuse bridges before its tanks, having failed to capture Allied fuel stocks, ran out of petrol. This represented the high-point of German success in the Ardennes.

On 23 December, American forces attacked northeast in order to relieve their forces encircled by the Germans at Bastogne, which they duly reached on 26 December. When the American commander of Bastogne received a German request to surrender his encircled troops he replied tersely, 'Nuts!'. From Christmas Day, American forces also forced the 2nd Panzer Division away from the Meuse bridges. At this point Field Marshal von Rundstedt, the

Top: An excellent view of the rear of a German Panzer V Panther medium tank that highlights the detail of the twin exhaust pipes and the extra stowage bins positioned on either side of them. The well-sloped nature of the upper hull sides is also clearly visible.

Above: American troops inspect an abandoned German Panther tank. One soldier is holding the barrel of the vehicle's 7.92mm MG 34 hull machine gun. The latter was absent in the first Panther Model D tanks, completed in early 1943, which rendered the vehicle vulnerable to close infantry attack.

Supreme German Army Commander in the West, decided that continuation of the offensive was futile, but Hitler insisted on further efforts to snatch success out of the jaws of defeat. The Führer ordered that on New Year's Day 1945, Manteuffel's Army – now reinforced by I SS Panzer Corps – undertake one final, desperate offensive effort around Bastogne.

To facilitate this renewed attempt, Hitler instructed von Rundstedt to launch a diversionary attack in Alsace-Lorraine on New Year's Eve 1944. Operation 'Northwind' involved a six-division thrust south towards Strasbourg to meet a southern pincer launched from the Colmar Pocket, the German-held salient that extended beyond the River Rhine onto French soil. The Germans hoped that their threat to Strasbourg would force the Americans to move reinforcements from the Ardennes region to Alsace-Lorraine. 'Northwind', however, achieved only limited tactical success and diverted few American forces away from the Ardennes. Consequently, the renewed German thrust in the Ardennes made little progress against ever-increasing Allied strength. On 3 January 1945, the Allies attacked the Fifth Panzer Army from both the northwest and southwest in an attempt to squeeze the German forces into extinction. Over the next 13 days, the Germans conducted a slow, fighting withdrawal back to their original start lines. During one month of

Above: A King Tiger of Kampfgruppe Peiper abandoned when the unit was encircled by the Allies at La Gleize. Just visible on the left of the hull glacis plate, above the mud-guard, is the crossed-keys insignia of the SS Leibstandarte Division.

intense combat in the Ardennes, Model's command lost 120,000 troops and 600 desperately needed AFVs, and as a result only meagre German forces now stood between the Allies and a successful advance across the River Rhine into the heart of the Reich itself.

In retrospect, the German Ardennes counteroffensive proved to be a costly, futile and ultimately disastrous gamble that threw away Germany's last, precious armoured reserves. Indeed, the Germans only managed to launch the counteroffensive through neglecting the needs of the Eastern Front. Consequently, in January 1945, renewed Soviet offensives easily ripped apart the German defensive positions in Poland. Ignoring the professional advice of his field commanders, Hitler's Ardennes counteroffensive constituted one of his greatest strategic follies. By 16 January 1945, the inevitable failure of the operation, and the consequent loss of irreplaceable military assets, ensured that it would only be a matter of months before Nazi Germany inevitably succumbed to defeat at the hands of the Allies.

CHAPTER 9
LAST STAND, 1945

By 1945, the German Army was being inexorably forced back by repeated Allied offensives. With all available armour thrown into the fray, the panzer arm succumbed amid the maelstrom that engulfed Nazi Germany.

Left: By 1945 the Soviets were producing thousands of armoured vehicles to augment the drive on Berlin. Here, heavy assault guns are being constructed at a former tractor factory.

Above: During the last 18 months of the war, German infantry relied increasingly on bicycles since Allied air power virtually precluded the safe movement of vehicles by day.

At the beginning of 1945 Germany's strategic position was disastrous. The mighty coalition of nations arrayed against the Nazis now stood on German soil. The German armed forces had suffered enormous losses in bitter, protracted, attritional warfare in multiple theatres that had bled them dry. The panzer arm in particular suffered heavy attrition in desperate defensive actions, plus in the December 1944 Ardennes counteroffensive in the West, during which the Germans lost another 600 armoured fighting vehicles (AFVs). Hitler had also taken the calculated gamble of denuding the Eastern Front of armour during the

autumn of 1944 in order to build up a reserve for the Ardennes assault. During November and December 1944, for example, the Eastern Front received just 921 tanks in comparison to some 2299 tanks despatched to the Western Front. It had been Hitler's original intention, after success in the Ardennes, to transfer the bulk of the German armour on the Western Front back to the East in time to meet the anticipated Soviet winter offensive. Though, in late January 1945, Hitler did withdraw the Sixth SS Panzer Army, which contained the bulk of the German armour in the West, he despatched it to Hungary to participate in a counteroffensive

Above: *German infantrymen, with white winter over-smocks, stand in front of a StuG III assault gun in the snow-covered fields of Poland during the January 1945 Soviet Vistula–Oder Offensive.*

Right: *A column of King Tiger tanks move across snow-covered open grasslands in preparation for the German 'Spring Awakening' Offensive in Hungary during early March 1945.*

intended to relieve Budapest, which had been encircled since Christmas Eve 1944.

To compensate for diminished armoured strength on the Eastern Front, the Germans introduced a new panzer corps organisation during November 1944 to streamline and enhance the effectiveness of the remaining panzer forces. This reorganisation permanently linked two panzer divisions under a corps command and amalgamated their service tails at corps level. The net result of restructuring was smaller and leaner armoured corps that packed greater punch. However, the Germans only had the time and resources to convert three tank corps – the XXIV, *Feldherrnehalle* and *Grossdeutschland* – to the new organisation prior to the onset of the Russian winter offensive in January 1945. Germany's hopes of repelling the Soviet steamroller rested on these meagre armoured reserves.

In early January 1945, Colonel-General Harpe's Army Group A fielded only six mechanised divisions and some 1136 tanks and assault guns to defend the Vistula Front in Poland. In fact, so weak was Army Group A relative to the mighty Soviet armada that stood against it – the Soviets deployed 4529 tanks opposite Harpe's command – that Heinz Guderian gloomily likened the Eastern Front to a pack of cards waiting to be knocked down. Events were to prove him correct, for on 12 January the Soviets launched a massive offensive across the River Vistula that sought to advance on a broad front to the Oder. With 163 divisions and 7042 tanks and assault guns, the Soviets enjoyed a marked numerical superiority. Massing their strength in the three Vistula bridgeheads which they had gained the previous September, and utilising highly successful deception operations, the Red Army gained surprise and quickly overwhelmed the thinly spread German infantry units holding the front. Soviet armoured reserves echeloned in depth quickly pushed through the gaps punched in the German front, and raced deep into the German rear to dislocate their command, control and communications.

Red whirlwind

The forward-deployed German defenders suffered such losses from a combination of massive artillery bombardment and concentrated frontal attacks, that they became badly depleted and were unable to fall back and hold the series of prepared rear defensive positions constructed during the autumn. With the front thus broken, the main weight of German countermeasures inevitably fell on General Nehring's XXIV Panzer Corps, with its 16th and 17th Panzer Divisions. But it could do little against the enormous mass of Soviet armour that surged forward, and it was rapidly swept up in the maelstrom of the Soviet advance on Kielce. Nevertheless, Nehring's armour did successfully shield the remnants of the Fourth Panzer Army as it desperately retreated to

Above: Two German soldiers mount a careful watch of the buildings in the distance for signs of the enemy. Their vehicle is a Sdkfz 251 mSPW armoured personnel carrier, and its firepower is provided by a frontal MG 34 machine gun.

Lodz to avoid encirclement. Cut off by the Soviet spearheads on 18 January, Nehring's command formed a wandering pocket behind Soviet lines that fought its way westwards.

Farther north, the inability of the 19th and 25th Panzer Divisions to halt the break-out of the First Byelorussian Front from the Magnuszew bridgehead led Hitler to order, on 15 January 1945, the transfer of the *Grossdeutschland* Panzer Corps, with the *Hermann Göring* Parachute Panzer Division and the *Brandenburg* Panzergrenadier Division, from East Prussia to the threatened Vistula Front. But these fresh armoured reserves represented too little, too late. By the time the corps began to detrain, the Soviets had already achieved a strategic breakthrough which hit the German formation while still in the process of redeploying, and dispersed it, preventing its assembly for a concentrated counterattack.

In the meantime, Nehring's panzer corps spent four days battling through the enemy to reach the hastily formed German front held by the *Grossdeutschland* Corps on the River Warthe. Nehring's troops had retreated 254km (120 miles) in 11 days of hard fighting, but his determined opposition had at least preserved

part of the Fourth Panzer Army. Nehring's losses had, however, been enormous, including all of his tanks. Further setbacks followed: in late January the Soviet Third Guards Tank Army overran the Upper Silesian industrial region and established bridgeheads over the Oder both north and south of Breslau on the 29th. The depleted *Grossdeutschland* and XXIV Panzer Corps made repeated counterattacks to eliminate the Steinau bridgehead, but lacked the strength to roll up the Soviet lodgement and the Germans had to revert to the defensive on 2 February.

The Red Army pounds Silesia

Only in Pomerania, on the northern flank of the Soviet offensive, did the Germans retain a coherent defence. Yet despite their spirited resistance, they could only watch as farther south Soviet armour raced to the Oder. On 1 February, three Soviet armies established bridgeheads on the west bank of the river, just 70km (32 miles) from Berlin. Yet no sooner had they reached the Oder, than the momentum of the Soviet advance petered out as the spearheads ran short of supplies, and as an early, sudden thaw melted the hitherto frozen river, hampering Soviet crossing efforts. The continued strong resistance being offered by German forces on the exposed northern flank of the Soviet penetration in Pomerania, as well as astride the River Neisse amid the Sudeten mountains on the southern flank in Silesia, also exerted a brake on Soviet forward momentum. Consequently, the Soviets halted their

advance at the Oder and instead attempted to eliminate the German threats to their flanks.

On 8 February, the Red Army renewed its efforts to roll up the German southern flank in Silesia held by the depleted Fourth Panzer Army. Initially it achieved dramatic successes, and by 15 February Breslau, the Silesian capital, had been encircled. But thereafter the advance quickly lost momentum as the Germans conducted a resolute defence of their homeland in the highly defensible Sudeten mountains. On 14 February, the hastily replenished XXIV and *Grossdeutschland* Panzer Corps counterattacked and temporarily cut off the Soviet Fourth Tank Army. After two days' hard fighting, however, the enemy broke through the German ring and retreated to form a new front farther east. Once again aggressive counteroffensive action by the two much-weakened panzer corps had shored up the southern flank.

With the southern sector restabilised, on 14 February the 19th Panzer Division launched an effort to relieve the encircled garrison of Breslau. But after establishing a tenuous link to the garrison, Sovi-

Above: A front view of a StuG III assault gun with whitewash camouflage seeking cover in a snow-covered copse. The inclusion of the large V-shaped gun mantlet instead of the Saukopf version identifies this as a vehicle constructed prior to spring 1944.

et countermeasures quickly severed the corridor anew the following day, and built a solid defensive front that denied the Germans any further progress. Instead, Field Marshall Schörner, commanding Army Group Centre, planned a limited counteroffensive against the more weakly defended Lauban sector in early March. Again the *Grossdeutschland* and XXIV Panzer Corps launched a classic pincer operation to recapture the strategic rail line that ran through Lauban. Launched during the night of 1/2 March, the Germans gained surprise, and on 5 March 1945 the *Führer* Grenadier Division and 8th Panzer Division linked up east of the town, and proceeded to annihilate much of the Soviet Third Tank Army.

Flush with victory, Schörner launched a similar counterattack at Striegau on 9 March, but the combination of inadequate

Above: *The Jagdpanzer V Jagdpanther was an elegantly shaped tank destroyer which possessed well-sloped armour, a low silhouette, a lethal 88mm gun and excellent mobility, attributes which made it a formidable fighting vehicle.*

Top *Frontal view of two 1944-vintage StuG III assault guns with Saukopf mantlets and additional frontal armour.*
Note also the gun shields on top of the turret for the close defence machine gun – although in this case both guns are missing.

Above: Close-up view of a Panzer V Panther turret. This view illustrates well the raised commander's cupola and the anti-aircraft MG 34 machine gun fitted on a special mounting. Note also the Zimmerit finish on the turret front.

strength, a forewarned enemy and bitter winter weather prevented a repeat of the success at Lauban. Striegau was eventually recaptured on 14 March, but only after a grim and costly attritional battle that the Germans could ill afford. Indeed, the following day the Soviet Fourth Ukrainian Front launched a new offensive against the First Panzer Army in Upper Silesia that aimed to capture the High Tatra Mountains of eastern Slovakia. The Red Army initiated its own pincer movement, which linked up at Neustadt on 18 March, surrounding much of the First Panzer Army. But once again it was the 16th Panzer Division of XXIV Panzer Corps that saved the day and freed most of the trapped troops. This latest triumph gained Nehring promotion to command of the First Panzer Army on 22 March, and under his leadership the Germans retained a strong and coherent defence in the Sudeten Mountains until late April 1945.

The stubborn, tenacious defence the Germans offered both in Silesia and in Pomerania bought Germany precious extra weeks of existence, and delayed the final Soviet drive on Berlin. On the northern flank, the Germans took advantage of the temporary exhaustion of the enemy to launch one last significant spoiling attack against the Soviets, at Stargard, to relieve the embattled garrison of Arnswalde. Operation 'Solstice' began on 15 February 1945, led by SS-Gruppenführer (Lieutenant-General) Steiner's Eleventh SS Panzer Army with eight mechanised divisions.

Achieving surprise, Steiner's forces broke through and relieved Arnswalde, but the momentum of the advance quickly dissipated, and on 17 February the Germans abandoned the operation. But the victory was short-lived: on 1 March the First Byelorussian Front launched a massive attack northwards that overran the German defences in eastern Pomerania and cleared the east bank of the Oder up to the Baltic coast. The Red Army had eliminated the threat to its northern flank and now turned its attention once again on Berlin.

The failure of 'Spring Awakening'

Meanwhile, the Sixth SS Panzer Army had redeployed to Hungary to close the last 34km (15 miles) that separated IV SS Panzer Corps from Budapest after its abortive January offensive. On 17 February, I SS Panzer Corps rapidly overran the enemy's Hron bridgehead over the Danube, but this proved to be the panzer arm's last major operational victory. On 5 March, the Sixth SS Panzer and Sixth Armies launched Operation 'Spring Awakening' with 11 panzer divisions and 877 AFVs. But the Soviets were forewarned of German intentions, and strongly reinforced their defences. The result was that in a series of bitter attacks, Germany's last armoured reserves were burnt out anew in a desperate attempt to save an already doomed city. Indeed, German losses exceeded 500 AFVs. When the offensive stalled, the garrison was forced to attempt a break-out in desperate circumstances. The result was a terrifying blood bath, during which only 785 of the defenders fought their way back to German lines.

On 14 March, the Red Army went over to the counteroffensive in Hungary and quickly drove back the depleted Waffen-SS

Above: This Panther tank has a fitting for an anti-aircraft machine gun on its turret cupola, but the actual weapon is missing. Note also the large, well-sloped hull glacis plate with single MG 34 for close defence.

Left: Side view of a Panzer V Panther concealed behind a wooden building with a thatched roof; the tank is accompanied by a lone German panzergrenadier. Note the almost hemispherical shape of the mantlet and the large road wheels.

troops. Furious at the failure of his favourite SS formations, Hitler ordered the SS troopers stripped of their formation cuff titles. During late March, the Soviets broke through the demoralised German troops and dashed for Vienna, the Austrian capital, as well as Prague, the former capital of Czechoslovakia. The SS panzers fought a brief and hopeless struggle to deny Vienna to the Soviets, but were forced to evacuate the city on 10 April.

Back in Germany, the end approached as the Nazi defences crumbled during the last two months of the war. The last major battle fought by Germany's heavy Tiger tanks occurred in early April 1945, when the instructors and recruits of SS armoured training units based at Sennelager, Westphalia, mobilised for combat in the wake of the American break-out from the Rhine

bridgehead, and the rapid pincer advance that encircled Army Group B in the Ruhr Pocket. Styling themselves the SS Armoured Replacement Brigade *Westphalia*, the SS soldiers offered bitter resistance to the American advance at Paderborn. Its 10 King Tiger and seven Tiger I tanks fought briefly but abortively to prevent the encirclement of Army Group B, before the brigade made a fighting retreat into the Harz Mountains, where, out of fuel and munitions, the remnants capitulated on 21 April 1945.

Committing the last remnants

The last significant German armoured attack of the war in the West was launched in mid-April 1945 by the newly raised Panzer Division *Clausewitz*. Despite its impressive-sounding name, the division was but a shadow of the great panzer divisions of the early war years. Hastily raised from armoured troop schools and various miscellaneous units, it fielded no more than 25 tanks of various models and possessed little cohesion. On 14 April, Hitler ordered *Clausewitz* to attack astride the boundary line dividing Anglo-American forces, and drive into the open flank of the American forces advancing towards the Elbe. Though the division initially made good progress against light opposition, once Allied reserves redeployed to counter the German push the division became bogged down in bitter defensive fighting. After a short struggle,

the division, having exhausted its fuel and munitions, was smashed on 21 April at Wittingen and effectively ceased to exist.

April 1945 saw the parallel disintegration of the Eastern Front as well. The diversion of German strength to Hungary ensured that the Ninth Army of Army Group Vistula could mass only 512 AFVs in its effort to thwart the final Soviet onslaught on Berlin, which began on 16 April. One of the last, big armoured battles of the war in the East occurred on the Seelow Heights east of Berlin on 18 April, as the Red Army broke through the German River Oder defences and advanced towards the German capital. At Buckow that day, the Panthers of the 11th SS Panzer Regiment and the Tigers of the 503rd SS Heavy Tank Battalion ambushed a Soviet armoured regiment and smashed it, leaving 50 burning Soviet tanks on the battlefield. Similarly, the Panzer Division *Muncheberg* caught another Soviet armoured regiment at Diedersdorf, leaving several dozen wrecked Soviet tanks. Likewise, on the reverse slope of the Seelow Heights the *Kurmark* Panzergrenadier Division and the 502nd SS Heavy Tank Battalion savaged the 8th Guards Mechanised Corps. These successes were to prove to be one of the last triumphs of the panzer arm. Despite the ferocity of their defence and the heavy losses inflicted on the enemy, the Germans gained a pyrrhic victory since

Left: A detailed view of the interior and the driver of a late-war German tank, possibly a Tiger. This picture shows clearly the heavily protected driver's vision slit, steering wheel and, to the right, the driving instrumentation gauges.

Right: Inside of a German armoured fighting vehicle showing the gunner and the firing mechanism of the main armament. Given the semi-open-topped nature of this vehicle, it is probably a German self-propelled gun of mid-war vintage.

Below: A dozen German infantrymen dismount from a Panther tank after hitching a lift in March or April 1945. At the front of the vehicle, one of the crew appears to be handing an MG 42 to the soldier with ammunition strung round his neck.

they still lost most of the heights that day, sealing the fate of Berlin.

The final battle for Berlin involved no more than 70 tanks of the *Muncheberg* Panzer and the 18th and 25th Panzergrenadier Divisions. These were reinforced by the last 31 assault guns produced on the Alkett assembly lines at Spandau, before that too was overrun by the Soviet advance. The refitting 249th Assault Gun Brigade received these brand-new vehicles on 24 April, and its successful break-in to Berlin in late April stands out as one of the few success stories during the death throes of the German Army in the last month of the war. The brigade joined action on 25 April at Spandau against advancing Red Army spearheads. But the next day it withdrew to Krampnitz for commitment to the Elbe Front against the Americans, who were fast approaching from the west. These orders were countermanded, however, when it became apparent that the Americans had decided not to advance past the River Elbe, the agreed demarcation line between the Soviet and Western Allied occupation zones of Germany. Consequently, the 249th Brigade returned to Berlin on 27 April to find that the Soviets had encircled the city. The brigade immediately counterattacked, and broke through the Soviet encircling ring before the Red Army had been able to consolidate its positions, and the brigade's assault guns took up defensive positions within the Berlin defensive perimeter. Reduced by 30 April to just nine operational assault guns, the brigade conducted a fighting retreat back

Above: One of the King Tiger tanks used by the Germans to support Operation 'Panzerfaust', SS-Standartenführer (Colonel) Otto Skorzeny's October 1944 military coup against Germany's wavering Axis satellite, Hungary.

Right: The last panzer battle is over: triumphant Soviet troops positioned in front of the Brandenburg Gate celebrate their conquest of Berlin and the death of their arch-enemy, the German Führer, Adolf Hitler.

to the Alexanderplatz. On 1 May, its remnants made their last stand at the Berlin Technical High School, and during the night of 2/3 May, after word reached it of Hitler's suicide and the imminent surrender of the garrison, the remainder of the brigade attempted to break out of Berlin, spearheaded by its last three remaining assault guns. These were quickly knocked out and the break-out stalled just outside Spandau. Amazingly, small groups of assault gun crews, including the brigade commander, managed to evade capture and infiltrated through Soviet lines to reach the River Elbe and surrender to American forces.

In early May 1945, all that remained of the armoured force was a shadow of its former self. The remaining German forces in northern Germany capitulated to the Western Allies on 5 May, and on 8 May 1945 the battered remnants of the panzer force laid down its arms and went into captivity.

BIBLIOGRAPHY

Bethell, Nigel, *The War Hitler Won: the Fall of Poland 1939* (New York, Holt, Rinehart & Winston, 1972)

Butler, Rupert, *The Black Angels: The Story of the Waffen-SS* (London, Sheridan, 1978)

Carell, Paul, *Invasion – They're Coming!* (London, Ballantine, 1962)

Carell, Paul, *Hitler Moves East, 1941–1943* (Boston, Little, Brown & Co., 1964)

Cooper, Matthew, *The German Army 1939–45: Its Military and Political Failure* (London, Macdonald & Jane's, 1978)

Corum, James. S., *The Roots of Blitzkrieg: Hans von Seeckt and German Military Reform* (Lawrence, KS, Kansas University Press, 1992)

Edwards, Roger, *Panzer: A Revolution in Warfare, 1939–1945* (London, Arms and Armour Press, 1989)

Ellis, Chris and Doyle, Hilary, *Panzerkampfwagen* (Kings Langley, Herts, Bellona, 1976)

Elstob, Peter, *Hitler's Last Offensive* (London, Corgi, 1972)

Erickson, John, *The Road to Stalingrad,* (New York, Harper & Row, 1976)

Erickson, John, *The Road to Berlin* (Boulder CO, Westview Press, 1983)

Feist, Uwe, *Deutsche Panzer 1917–1945,* (Fallbrook, CA, Aero Publishers, 1978)

Fürbringer, Herbert, *9SS-Panzer Division Hohenstaufen 1944: Normandie-Tarnopol-Arnhem* (Paris, Editions Heimdal, 1984)

Gilbert, Adrian, *Waffen-SS: An Illustrated History* (London, Guild Publishing, 1989)

Grove, Eric, *German Armour 1939-1940: Poland and France* (New Malden, Almark, 1976)

Guderian, Heinz, *Panzer Leader* (London, Futura, 1974)

Harris, J.P. and Toase, F.H. (Eds.), *Armoured Warfare,* (London, Batsford, 1990)

Hastings, Max, *Das Reich* (London, Michael Joseph, 1981)

Irving, David, *The Trail of the Fox* (London, Weidenfeld & Nicolson, 1977)

Keegan, John, *Waffen-SS: The Asphalt Soldiers* (London, Ballantine, 1970)

Kershaw, Robert J., *It Never Snows in September: the German View of Market Garden & the Battle of Arnhem, September 1944* (Marlborough, Crowood Press, 1990)

Lefevre, Eric, *Panzers in Normandy: Then and Now* (London, Battleline Books, 1984)

Lefevre, Eric, *Battle of the Bulge: Then and Now* (London, Battle of Britain Ltd, 1984)

Lucas, James, *Panzer Army Africa* (London, MacDonald & Jane's, 1977)

Lucas, James, *Last Days of the Reich: the Collapse of Nazi Germany, May 1945* (London, Grafton, 1987)

Lucas, James, *Das Reich* (London, Arms & Armour, 1991)

Luck, Colonel Hans von, *Panzer Commander: The Memoirs of Hans von Luck* (London, Praeger, 1989)

MacDonald, C.B., *The Battle of the Bulge* (London, Weidenfeld & Nicholson, 1984)

Manstein, Erich von, *Lost Victories* (Chicago, H. Regency Co., 1958)

Mellenthin, F.W. von, *Panzer Battles 1939–45* (London, Cassell, 1955)

Nowarra, Heinz. J., *German Tanks 1914–1968* (New York, Arco, 1968)

Quarrie, Bruce, *Hitler's Samurai: the Waffen-SS in Action* (Wellingborough, Patrick Stephens, 1986)

Quarrie, Bruce, *Hitler's Teutonic Knights: SS Panzers in Action* (Wellingborough, Patrick Stephens, 1986)

Reynolds, Michael, *Steel Inferno: I SS Panzer Corps in Normandy* (New York, Sarpedon, 1997)

Senger und Etterlin, Ferdinand M., *German Tanks of World War II* (Harrisburg, PA, Stackpole Books, 1969)

Stein, George H., *The Waffen-SS: Hitler's Elite Guard at War 1939–45* (New York, Cornell, 1966)

Strawson, John, *The Battle for North Africa* (New York, C. Scribners, 1969)

Toland, John, *The Last One Hundred Days* (London, Arthur Baker, 1965)

Turnbull, Patrick, *The Spanish Civil War 1936–39* (London, Osprey, 1978)

Williamson, Gordon, *SS: The Blood-Soaked Soil* (London, Brown Books, 1995)

Zaloga, Stephen, and Madej, Victor, *The Polish Campaign 1939* (New York, Hippocrene, 1985)

Ziemke, Earl F., *Stalingrad to Berlin* (Washington, GPO, 1968)

Ziemke, Earl F., *Moscow to Stalingrad* (Washington, GPO, 1987)

INDEX

Page numbers in *italics* refer to captions.

PICTURE CREDITS

All photographs Christopher Ailsby Historical Archives except the following:

Bundesarchiv: 152 (both)
TRH Pictures: 22, 25, 30 (top), 36-37, 39, 42-43, 43, 44, 45, 46 (bottom),
47 (both), 48-49, 50 (both), 51, 52 (both), 52-53, 53, 54, 54-55, 55, 56 (bottom), 57 (both),
60, 61, 62 (both), 63 (bottom), 66, 66-67, 67, 68, 69 (bottom), 70 (top), 70-71, 72 (both), 76, 80, 80-81, 81, 98 (top),
110-111, 128, 129, 130, 138, 142 (bottom), 147, 154 (top), 156 (top), 157 (top), 159, 160, 161, 173
TRH Pictures via Espadon: 40, 74, 78, 121, 127